D1524494

JOIN THE JOURNEY JUNIOR

FROM GENESIS TO JESUS | VOLUME 2
DAILY BIBLE STUDY

JOIN THE JOURNEY

JOIN THE JOURNEY JR.

READ

Bible Reading Plan: Find this year's plan and the New Living Translation at JoinTheJourney.com!

LISTEN

Weekly Podcast: Every Friday we've got a new podcast episode for families just like yours, filled with fun stories, discussion questions, and more! You can even listen with your younger siblings. Just ask your parent or a trusted Christian friend to search for "Join The Journey Junior" wherever they listen to podcasts.

WRITE

Guided Journals: If you're reading this, you've got one! But do your friends? Join The Journey Junior journals are available on Amazon.

JOIN THE JOURNEY
(FOR GROWN UPS)

READ

Reading the Bible Together: Find the Bible reading plan, daily devotionals, and discussion questions at JoinTheJourney.com.

LISTEN

Daily Podcast: Dive deeper into each day's passage in 10 minutes or less. Just search for "Join The Journey."

WRITE

Guided Journals: Journals for parents and older siblings are available on Amazon! Just search for "From Genesis to Jesus, Vol. 2."

ENCOURAGEMENT
TO PARENTS

Congrats on making it halfway through the year reading God's Word as a family. We pray that God's Word has been a central topic of discussion and even application. For the second half of the year, we will be reading through 1 & 2 Samuel, 1 & 2 Kings, Ezra, and Nehemiah ... all leading up to a celebration of Advent at the end of the year.

Now you might be wondering why we are spending so much time in the Old Testament when the official Christ-followers began in the New Testament. See if this helps...

Imagine picking up a book you've never read before and starting in the middle. How often would you feel lost or like you missed some important information from earlier? There would be people, events, and the developing storyline that you would have missed out on. While it's often tempting for us to read from the Gospels onward, what if I told you that the New Testament writers quoted or alluded to the Old Testament over 300 times? Would that change how you feel about the importance of the first half of the Bible? In fact, a tenth of Jesus's words were taken from 49 different Old Testament verses! He even explained to two of His disciples that He can be seen in the Old Testament: "Then Jesus took them through the writings of Moses and all the prophets, explaining from all the Scriptures the things concerning himself" (Luke 24:27).

So, learning and listening to the stories from before Jesus's birth highlights God's unfolding rescue plan, sets the stage for the Gospels, and finally helps us grasp all the references made to believers about Old Testament events.

Keep pressing on and keep passing on your faith!

Chris Sherrod
Family & Marriage Director
csherrod@watermark.org

3

WELCOME TO THE
ADVENTURE
OF READING THROUGH THE BIBLE!

Adventure?? Are we talking about the same thing? As Han Solo would say, "It's true. All of it."

Believe it or not, the Bible is an exciting book given by God to understand Him and His salvation plan for us through Jesus. This is because the greatest adventure comes through knowing and following God!

The Bible is absolutely true, never changes, and teaches us how to follow Jesus. Here are some amazing things God's Word is compared to:

- It's like a *lamp* that guides your steps at night (Psalm 119:105)
  (Picture an explorer in a cave with a torch that lights up the whole place, leading him to gold.)

- It's like *delicious food* that makes you happy (Jeremiah 15:16)
  (Yep, they just compared the Bible to pizza. Extra cheese, double pepperoni, stuffed crust, the works.)

- It's like *water* that cleans you up (Ephesians 5:26)
  (Like being at a waterpark where you can also get your shower in for the week.)

- It's like a *sword* used for battle (Ephesians 6:17)
  (Lightsaber, samurai sword, Thor's hammer, you name it.)

- It's like a *mirror* that shows what you look like (James 1:22-25)
  (Not like one of those fun house mirrors. It's a mirror that shows you who you truly are.)

Because reading the Bible is one of the most important ways to grow your relationship with Jesus, *Join The Journey Jr.* is here to help you start forming the daily habit of spending time in God's Word. Along the way, talk with your parent, grandparent, or trusted Christian friend about what you're learning, and feel free to ask lots of questions! You might even want to listen together.

I'm so glad you're joining your family and church on The Journey!

Sean Hill
Watermark Kids Director

TABLE OF CONTENTS

UNDERSTANDING
THE BIBLE

Have you ever been to a library? Maybe there's one at your school or in your city.

I want you to think about a library you've visited recently. I bet there were a LOT of books!

How many books do you think were in that library? _____

All the books in that library probably had little stickers or barcodes on them—library books are very organized, and that organization is part of what makes libraries so great!

But what if the library wasn't organized? What if all the stickers and barcodes were removed? Rather than being kept on shelves, what if the books were in piles all over the room? What if, when you wanted to find that new comic book, all you could find were your mom's cookbooks??

Just like a library contains neatly organized books that tell stories or share information, the Bible is one big book that contains a lot of smaller books that tell stories and share information. But these books? And these stories? They're much better than anything a library could offer, because they aren't just simple human words – they're God's words! **The Bible is a bunch of smaller stories that point to one big, true story – the story of God and His rescue plan through Jesus.**

1

SO HOW IS THE BIBLE ORGANIZED??

This big story of the Bible is divided into halves, and the halves are divided into books, and the books are divided into chapters, and the chapters are divided into verses! This makes it SO much easier to find what you're looking for in the Bible!

Here are some other fun facts about the Bible:

- There are 66 books in the Bible
- The Bible was written by more than 40 different authors who put God's words on paper (2 Peter 1:16-21)
- The Bible was originally written in three different languages
- The Bible does not contain any mistakes
- The Bible is absolutely true! It is **NOT** made up!

SO HOW DO I USE THE BIBLE'S ORGANIZATION SYSTEM?

When you're at church on Sunday, you might hear a teacher or pastor talk about a specific book of the Bible. Let's pretend our teacher asks us to turn in our Bibles to **John 3:16**.

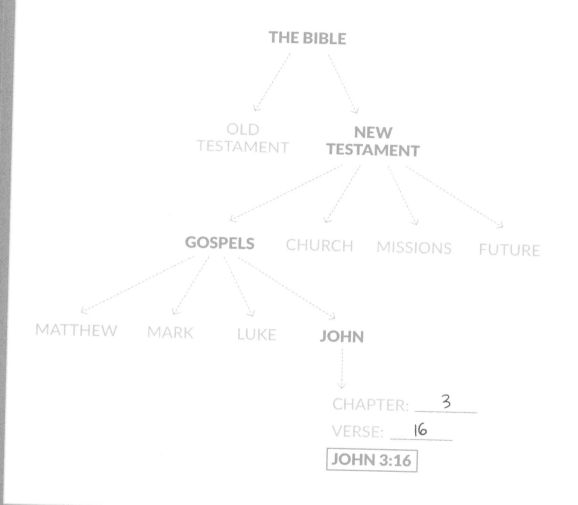

THE BIBLE

OLD TESTAMENT · **NEW TESTAMENT**

GOSPELS · CHURCH · MISSIONS · FUTURE

MATTHEW · MARK · LUKE · **JOHN**

CHAPTER: ___3___

VERSE: ___16___

JOHN 3:16

Pro tip: If you're having trouble finding a book of the Bible, there should be a table of contents at the beginning of your Bible.

Much like a library, our Bibles are organized to help us find the same books and verses our friends and family are reading so we can talk about them. By the way, reading the Bible is easier and better when we all do it together!

WAIT, SO WHAT'S THE DEAL WITH "TRANSLATIONS"?

Think about it kind of like this: If you have younger siblings, I bet you use words they don't understand. For example, when you catch your baby sibling eating that day-old Cheerio from the floor, you could say, "That's yucky!" Or, you could say, "That's disgusting!" Your baby sibling might not understand what "disgusting" means, but I bet they know the word "yucky!" You're still saying mostly the same thing, just with a word your sibling understands.

Similarly, different Bibles communicate God's Word through several "translations." Different Bible translations tell the same stories, but some of them use words that are harder to understand. Join The Journey Jr. uses the New Living Translation (NLT for short). If you don't have an NLT Bible, the one you have will still work great! You might have a little trouble with some of the activities, but no worries! Just ask a trusted Christian friend for help!

Don't let the size of the Bible scare you away. All the books of the Bible, together, form **ONE BIG STORY**. It's all about **God's people** (from Adam and Eve, to Israel, and the Church) **in God's place** (first Eden, then the Promised Land, and later the New Creation) **under God's rule**! As we read from Genesis to Jesus, we'll discover that God rules over all things! He's the One in charge.

This year, we will be reading stories from the first half of the Bible, the Old Testament. These books will help us understand God's story and answer questions like: When did the story start? Why do we need Jesus? What even happened before Jesus came?

The Old Testament is full of exciting characters: amazing leaders, kings and princesses, warriors who fight in dangerous battles, kids who do BIG things for God, and also a lot of people who make bad choices. But God used all these people to accomplish His goals, and He's still using them to teach us today!

BIBLE TIMELINE

Throughout this journal, you'll see special icons that help us recall where on the Bible Timeline specific passages take place in relation to the rest of the story. The Bible Timeline is an outline for the whole entire Bible—all 66 books!

Remember: The Bible is the written Word of God. It was true then, it's true now, and it will be true forever. The Bible tells the story of God's people, the need for His Son, and His plan for the world.

Turn the page to see all the icons and their explanations. Come back to the Bible Timeline while you are reading to remind yourself where you are in the story of the whole Bible.

1. CREATION GOD CREATES EVERYTHING!

GENESIS 1-3, JOB

2. PATRIARCHS STORIES THAT MARK THE FAITH FAMILY TREE

GENESIS 4-50

3. EXODUS ESCAPING SLAVERY, THEN A NATION SET APART

EXODUS, LEVITICUS, NUMBERS

4. CONQUEST MOVING INTO THE PROMISED LAND

DEUTERONOMY, JOSHUA

5. JUDGES UNIQUELY NEEDED RULERS FOR ISRAEL

JUDGES, RUTH

6. KINGDOM ISRAEL'S HIGHS AND LOWS

1 SAMUEL, 2 SAMUEL, PSALMS, 1 KINGS, PROVERBS, ECCLESIASTES,
SONG OF SOLOMON, 2 KINGS, ISAIAH, JEREMIAH, LAMENTATIONS, HOSEA,
JOEL, AMOS, OBADIAH, JONAH, MICAH, NAHUM, HABAKKUK, ZEPHANIAH,
1 CHRONICLES, 2 CHRONICLES

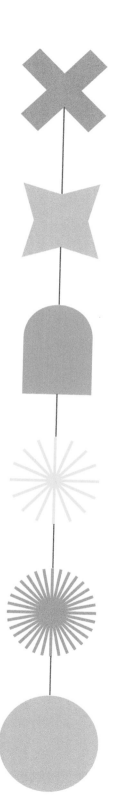

7. EXILE WHILE ISRAEL WAS BEING DISCIPLINED...

EZEKIEL, DANIEL

8. RETURN ISRAEL IS HOME AT LAST!

EZRA, HAGGAI, ZECHARIAH, ESTHER, NEHEMIAH, MALACHI

9. GOSPELS MEET THE HERO OF THE STORY!

MATTHEW, MARK, LUKE, JOHN

10. CHURCH GOD'S PEOPLE ARE EMPOWERED!

ACTS

11. MISSIONS LETTERS WRITTEN TO GOD'S PEOPLE

ROMANS, 1 CORINTHIANS, 2 CORINTHIANS, GALATIANS, EPHESIANS, PHILIPPIANS, COLOSSIANS, 1 THESSALONIANS, 2 THESSALONIANS, 1 TIMOTHY, 2 TIMOTHY, TITUS, PHILEMON, HEBREWS, JAMES, 1 PETER, 2 PETER, 1 JOHN, 2 JOHN, 3 JOHN , JUDE

12. FUTURE JESUS IS COMING BACK!

REVELATION

HOW TO STUDY
THE BIBLE

Reading the Bible helps us get to know and understand God as a close friend. We never want to only learn facts or stories from the Bible – we want a clearer picture of who God is, what He's done, and what He thinks about His creation!

Read Psalm 1:1-3 and draw a picture of the scene described.

[1] Oh, the joys of those who do not follow the advice of the wicked,
or stand around with sinners, or join in with mockers.

[2] But they delight in the law of the Lord, meditating on it day and night.

[3] They are like trees planted along the riverbank, bearing fruit each season.
Their leaves never wither, and they prosper in all they do.

-------------------------------- DRAW A PICTURE HERE --------------------------------

WANT SOME TIPS ON HOW TO STUDY THE BIBLE??

PRAY!

Ask God to help you stay focused and understand what you're reading. Ask Him to help you respond and, most importantly, fall more in love with Him, the God of the Bible! We'd encourage you to pray with your parents or a T.C.F.[1]

ASK: "WHAT?"

Every day you'll get a reading assignment. Try to read through each day's passage twice. Yes, you read that right...twice!! Reading through Scripture multiple times helps us stay focused, remember what we read, and helps us to have "listening ears."

Your goal is to know what's happening in what you're reading. Here's an easy way to think about it: Could I put what I just read in my own words and explain it to someone else? Don't worry yet about "What's God trying to teach me here?" Just start with "What's happening here?"

To help you out, each day we'll give you one observation question to complete. It will be a "Who, What, When, Where, Why, or How" question! We'll only give you one each day, but you can always answer more! In fact, most of the time it's really helpful to think about all of the questions on every passage we study.

If a parent or trusted Christian friend in your life is doing the adult version of Join The Journey, they'll have some different steps in their journal. A good question for you to ask them is, "What did you notice when you read today's passage?"

NEXT ASK: "SO WHAT?"

Now that you know what happened, think about why it matters. What is the "timeless truth" that God is trying to teach us? This part of Bible study is often called interpretation.

One key to correctly understanding (interpreting) Scripture is to make sure you don't ignore the context! Context is helpful information that clarifies the meaning of something.

If you're looking for the context behind a verse, ask three questions:
- When did this happen?[2]
- What verses come before this one?
- What verses come after this one?

Your answers to those three questions will help you make sure you are interpreting Scripture correctly! Because once you understand what you're reading, then you can apply it to your life![3]

---

[1] Trusted Christian Friend...this could be a parent, older sibling, Watermark Kids leader, or anyone that you think could help give you some more ways to think about this stuff!

[2] Not sure when something took place? Take a look at the Bible Timeline and make sure you know where this story fits into God's big story!

[3] Not sure how something applies to your life? Ask, "What was true then, what's true now, and what is always true?"

4 FINALLY ASK: "NOW WHAT?"

Now that you know what happened, why it matters, and what it means, simply apply it to your life! Ask yourself, "How can I live differently because of what I read?" Every day you will get one application question. These questions are meant to help you live out what God is teaching you through His Word.

God's Word is powerful! It helps us get to know God, identify our sins,[4] and live a life that honors God.

Remember, we never want to only learn facts or stories from the Bible. We want to spend time reading the Bible every day to strengthen our relationship with God so that we can know and love Him more. God's Word helps us better understand God's character (who He is), God's will (what He wants for us), and His way (how He wants us to think, speak, and act).

But the good news is, if you're a believer in Jesus' life, death, burial, and resurrection, you don't have to respond to God in your own strength! On our own, we are powerless to live a lifestyle that glorifies God. 1 Corinthians 15:57 says, "But thank God! He gives us victory over sin and death through our Lord Jesus Christ."

After Jesus rose from the grave, He told His disciples, "You will receive power when the Holy Spirit comes upon you. And you will be my witnesses, telling people about me everywhere—in Jerusalem, throughout Judea, in Samaria, and to the ends of the earth" (Acts 1:8). So what does this mean for us? When you give your life to Jesus, you receive the Holy Spirit! And the Holy Spirit[5] empowers us to obey God's Word.

5 PRAY!

Romans 8:1-2 says, "So now there is no condemnation for those who belong to Christ Jesus. And because you belong to him, the power of the life-giving Spirit has freed you from the power of sin that leads to death."

Sometimes, we make bad choices. We sin.

Becoming a Christian doesn't make you perfect, but it does change your heart. Believers want to honor God and say "No" to sin, but this can be way easier to say than to actually do. After you complete each day's reading, you'll see some space to write out a prayer. Spend some time asking God to help you respond to what you read in a way that honors Him. Writing out a prayer is like writing a letter to God. It can be so easy for our thoughts to wander, but writing it down can help us stay focused!

---

[4] Sin is anything we think, say, or do that doesn't please or honor God.
[5] God's Spirit is the Helper Jesus promised to send when He returned to heaven. When you believe in Jesus as your Savior, God gives you the Spirit as your confidence that you belong to God forever! The Holy Spirit helps you to know God's best and to live in a way that honors Him.

SPEND SOME TIME, RIGHT NOW, WRITING OUT A PRAYER TO GOD.

1. Thank Him for what He's done for you.

2. Tell God about your attitude. Do you want to read the Bible? Do you like reading? Are you glad you have this Bible study book?

3. Ask God to change your heart. Ask Him to help you want to read the Bible more and more. Ask God to deepen your love for Him.

JANUARY

- 02 Gen. 1:1-5
- 03 Gen. 1:26-31
- 04 Gen. 2:18-25
- 05 Gen. 3:1-15
- 06 Gen. 4:3-10
- 09 Gen. 6:11-22
- 10 Gen. 7:6-16
- 11 Gen. 9:9-17
- 12 Gen. 11:1-9
- 13 Gen. 12:10-20
- 16 Gen. 13:8-17
- 17 Gen. 14:8-16
- 18 Gen. 15:1-6
- 19 Gen. 17:1-8
- 20 Gen. 18:1-15
- 23 Gen. 19:12-26
- 24 Gen. 20:2-18
- 25 Gen. 21:1-7
- 26 Gen. 22:1-14
- 27 Gen. 24:12-27
- 30 Gen. 24:12-27
- 31 Gen. 26:1-9

FEBRUARY

- 01 Gen. 27:1-17
- 02 Gen. 27:18-29
- 03 Gen. 27:30-43
- 06 Gen. 28:10-22
- 07 Gen. 29:1-14
- 08 Gen. 30:22-32
- 09 Gen. 31:3-9
- 10 Gen. 31:32-42
- 13 Gen. 32:3-20
- 14 Gen. 33:1-14
- 15 Gen. 35:1-15
- 16 Gen. 37:1-17
- 17 Gen. 37:18-36
- 20 Gen. 39:19-23
- 21 Gen. 41:15-36
- 22 Gen. 41:37-57
- 23 Gen. 42:1-16
- 24 Gen. 43:19-34
- 27 Gen. 44:18-34
- 28 Gen. 45:1-15

MARCH

- 01 Gen. 46:1-7
- 02 Gen. 49:1-2, 49:8-12
- 03 Gen. 50:14-21
- 06 Exod. 1:6-22
- 07 Exod. 2:2-10, 2:23-25
- 08 Exod. 3:2-15
- 09 Exod. 5:1-9, 5:19-23
- 10 Exod. 6:1-13
- 13 Exod. 7:1-5, 7:10-22
- 14 Exod. 9:13-30, 9:34-35
- 15 Exod. 11:1-10
- 16 Exod. 12:21-32
- 17 Exod. 13:8-22
- 20 Exod. 14:16-31
- 21 Exod. 15:1-6, 15:19-21
- 22 Exod. 16:4-12
- 23 Exod. 17:1-7
- 24 Exod. 19:1-9
- 27 Exod. 20:2-17
- 28 Exod. 21:1, 22:5-12
- 29 Exod. 23:20-22, 23:25-32
- 30 Exod. 24:1-8
- 31 Exod. 25:1-9

APRIL

- 03 Zech. 9:9-13, Matt. 21:1-11
- 04 Exod. 12, Lk. 22:17-20
- 05 Isa. 53, Lk. 23:6-49
- 06 Num. 21:9, John 3:14-21
- 07 Isa. 25:7-8, Mark 16, 1 Cor. 15:54
- 10 Exod. 26:30-36
- 11 Exod. 27:20-28:5
- 12 Exod. 29:35-37, 29:42-46
- 13 Exod. 30:25-33
- 14 Exod. 31:16
- 17 Exod. 32:1-14
- 18 Exod. 32:15-20, 32:30-35
- 19 Exod. 33:12-23
- 20 Exod. 34:10-14, 34:29-35
- 21 Exod. 35:1-5a, 35:21-29
- 24 Exod. 36:1-8
- 25 Exod. 37:1-2, 37:17-24
- 26 Exod. 38:21-31
- 27 Exod. 39:32-43
- 28 Exod. 40:17-18, 40:34-38

MAY

- 01 Num. 1:1-19
- 02 Num. 3:5-16
- 03 Num. 4:1-20
- 04 Num. 5:1-10
- 05 Num. 6:1-8
- 08 Num. 7:1-11, 7:89
- 09 Num. 9:15-23
- 10 Num. 11:1-6, 11:10-15
- 11 Num. 11:18-20, 11:31-33
- 12 Num. 12:1-15
- 15 Num. 13:25-33
- 16 Num. 14:1-19
- 17 Num. 14:20-37
- 18 Num. 16:1-11
- 19 Num. 16:16-26
- 22 Num. 16:27-40
- 23 Num. 16:41-50
- 24 Num. 17:1-13
- 25 Num. 18:1-14
- 26 Num. 20:2-13
- 29 Num. 21:4-9
- 30 Num. 22:1-6
- 31 Num. 22:7-21

JUNE

- 01 Num. 22:22-38
- 02 Num. 23:1-12
- 05 Num. 24:1-14
- 06 Num. 24:15-25
- 07 Num. 27:12-23
- 08 Num. 33:50-56
- 09 Num. 34:1-15
- 12 Josh. 1:5-9
- 13 Josh. 2:1-11
- 14 Josh. 3:7-17
- 15 Josh. 5:13-15
- 16 Josh. 6:1-20
- 19 Josh. 7:1-12
- 20 Josh. 8:1-23
- 21 Josh. 8:24-35
- 22 Josh. 9:3-15
- 23 Josh. 10:7-14
- 26 Josh. 10:34-42
- 27 Josh. 11:4-20
- 28 Josh. 13:1-7
- 29 Josh. 14:6-15
- 30 Josh. 17:14-18

- 03 Josh. 18:1-10
- 04 Josh. 20:1-9
- 05 Josh. 23:1-13
- 06 Josh. 23:14-16
- 07 Josh. 24:14-28
- 10 Jdg. 1:19- 25, 1:28
- 11 Jdg. 2:6-13
- 12 Jdg. 4:1-15
- 13 Jdg. 6:34-40
- 14 Jdg. 7:1-18
- 17 Jdg. 7:19-23
- 18 Jdg. 13:2-14
- 19 Jdg. 15:9-17
- 20 Jdg. 16:6-22
- 21 Jdg. 16:25-30
- 24 Jdg. 21:24-25
- 25 Ruth 1:1-18
- 26 Ruth 2:2-13, 2:17-20
- 27 Ruth 3:1-13
- 28 Ruth 4:9-17
- 31 1 Sam. 1:7-18

- 01 1 Sam. 2:1-10
- 02 1 Sam. 4:2-11
- 03 1 Sam. 5:6-12
- 04 1 Sam. 7:1-15
- 07 1 Sam. 8:1-9
- 08 1 Sam. 9:11-24
- 09 1 Sam. 10:1-13
- 10 1 Sam. 12:13-25
- 11 1 Sam. 13:5-15
- 14 1 Sam. 14:6-15
- 15 1 Sam. 15:1-3, 15:17-23
- 16 1 Sam. 16:1-13
- 17 1 Sam. 17:3-11, 17:24-27, 17:36-50
- 18 1 Sam. 18:5-12, 19:8-12
- 21 1 Sam. 20:12-22, 20:37-42
- 22 1 Sam. 21:1-9, 22:9-19
- 23 1 Sam. 23:1-5
- 24 1 Sam. 24:3-12, 24:16-20
- 25 1 Sam. 25:9-22, 25:32-35
- 28 1 Sam. 26:1-14, 26:17-18, 26:21-22
- 29 1 Sam. 27:1-28:2
- 30 1 Sam. 29:1-11
- 31 1 Sam. 29:1-8, 29:16-20

- 01 1 Sam. 31:1-13
- 04 2 Sam. 1:1-12
- 05 2 Sam. 2:1-11, 3:1, 3:17-19
- 06 2 Sam. 4:1-11
- 07 2 Sam. 5:1-15
- 08 2 Sam. 6:1-15
- 11 2 Sam. 7:1-17
- 12 2 Sam. 9:1-13
- 13 2 Sam. 10:9-19
- 14 2 Sam. 12:1-10
- 15 2 Sam. 14:1-14
- 18 2 Sam. 16:11-19, 17:5-18
- 19 2 Sam. 18:19-22, 18:33, 19:14-23
- 20 2 Sam. 20:1-2, 20:16-23
- 21 2 Sam. 22:1-4, 22:17-20, 22:29-36
- 22 2 Sam. 23:1-7, 24:9-17
- 25 1 Kgs. 1:28-37
- 26 1 Kgs. 2:1-12
- 27 1 Kgs. 3:5-15
- 28 1 Kgs. 4:20-34
- 29 1 Kgs. 5:1-12

- 02 1 Kgs. 6:11-22
- 03 1 Kgs. 7:45-51
- 04 1 Kgs. 8:1-11
- 05 1 Kgs. 9:1-9
- 06 1 Kgs. 10:1-10
- 09 1 Kgs. 11:1-13
- 10 1 Kgs. 12:1-20
- 11 1 Kgs. 12:25-33
- 12 1 Kgs. 14:1-17
- 13 1 Kgs. 16:25-34
- 16 1 Kgs. 17:1-24
- 17 1 Kgs. 18:1-19
- 18 1 Kgs. 18:20-40
- 19 1 Kgs. 19:1-21
- 20 1 Kgs. 20:35-43
- 23 1 Kgs. 21:20-29
- 24 2 Kgs. 1:1-17
- 25 2 Kgs. 2:1-14
- 26 2 Kgs. 2:15-25
- 27 2 Kgs. 4:8-17
- 30 2 Kgs. 4:18-37
- 31 2 Kgs. 8:16-27

- 01 2 Kgs. 9:1-13
- 02 2 Kgs. 10:28-32
- 03 2 Kgs. 17:6-23
- 06 2 Kgs. 18:1-12
- 07 2 Kgs. 21:1-18
- 08 2 Kgs. 22:1-2, 22:8-11, 23:1-3
- 09 2 Kgs. 23:24-27, 23:31-32, 23:36-37
- 10 2 Kgs. 24:1-13; 25:1-7, 25:1-24
- 13 Ezra 1:1-7
- 14 Ezra 3:1-13
- 15 Ezra 6:6-18
- 16 Ezra 7:6-10, 7:21-26, 8:21-23
- 17 Ezra 9:10-15, 10:1-2
- 20 Neh. 1:1-11
- 21 Neh. 2:4-20
- 22 Neh. 4:1-15
- 23 Neh. 5:9-19
- 24 Neh. 6:1-16
- 27 Neh. 8:1-12
- 28 Neh. 9:3-8, 9:29-38
- 29 Neh. 10:28-39
- 30 Neh. 12:27-43

- 01 Neh. 13:10-22
- 04 John 1:1-18
- 05 Gen. 1:1-2, 1:26-28, 3:1-15
- 06 Gen. 12:1-3, Deut. 18:18, Acts 3:17-26
- 07 Gen. 17:15-19, Rom. 9:1-13
- 08 Num. 24:17, Jer. 33:14-16, 2 Sam. 7:4-17
- 11 Isa. 9:2-7, Matt. 1:1-17
- 12 Isa. 7:14, Luke 1:6-7, 1:11-45
- 13 Luke 1:46-56
- 14 Luke 2:1-7
- 15 Luke 2:8-12
- 18 Luke 2:13-18
- 19 Luke 2:19-20
- 20 Mic. 5:2-5
- 21 Mic. 5:2, Matt. 2:1-6
- 22 Matt. 2:7-12
- 25 Luke 2:11-14
- 26 Rev. 1:4-7
- 27 Rev. 3:20-22
- 28 Rev. 22:12-13
- 29 Rev. 22:16-20

MONTHLY **MEMORY VERSES**

| JULY | "But the wisdom from above is first of all pure. It is also peace loving, gentle at all times, and willing to yield to others. It is full of mercy and the fruit of good deeds. It shows no favoritism and is always sincere." – James 3:17 |

| "For even the Son of Man came not to be served but to serve others and to give his life as a ransom for many." – Mark 10:45 | AUGUST |

| SEPTEMBER | "In the same way, let your good deeds shine out for all to see, so that everyone will praise your heavenly Father." – Matthew 5:16 |

| "Trust in the Lord with all your heart; do not depend on your own understanding. Seek his will in all you do, and he will show you which path to take." – Proverbs 3:5-6 | OCTOBER |

| NOVEMBER | "Always be joyful. Never stop praying. Be thankful in all circumstances, for this is God's will for you who belong to Christ Jesus." – 1 Thessalonians 5:16-18 |

| "Create in me a clean heart, O God. Renew a loyal spirit within me." – Psalm 51:10 | DECEMBER |

MARK 4:35-41 (EXAMPLE)

"Then he asked them, 'Why are you ___*afraid*___ ? Do you ___*still*___ have ___*no*___ ___*faith*___ ?'"

MARK 4:40

WHAT DO I NOTICE?
What's happening? Draw a picture **or** write 3 words that describe what you read!

storm

sleeping

faith

WHAT SHOULD I DO?
Do you see any bad examples? Who and why? Do you ever act like that bad example? Explain.

—The disciples were in a real panic, they forgot to have faith in Jesus. This is a bad example.

—Just like the disciples, I get really scared or nervous at certain times. Like when I have to talk in front of the class at school.

PRAYER:
Spend some time thinking about today's passage and write out a prayer to God. Ask Him to help you respond in the right way.

Dear God, I thank you for being so powerful that you can end storms. I pray that

I wouldn't be afraid and that I would remember you are in control. But if I do get

afraid, would you help me to run straight to you in prayer and remember this story?

Did you know Join The Journey Junior has a weekly podcast? You can listen to it in the car or at the breakfast table! Ask a parent or trusted Christian friend to help you subscribe so you don't miss an episode!

1 SAMUEL

Outward appearances can be deceiving. God looks at the heart.

HELPFUL HINTS:

- **God** – The all-powerful, all-knowing, all-seeing Creator of everything

- **Sin** – Anything we think, say, or do that does not please or honor God

- **Prayer** – Talking and listening to God

1 SAMUEL

1 SAMUEL 1:7-18

"Hannah was in deep anguish, crying bitterly as she prayed to the Lord."

1 SAMUEL 1:10

WHAT DO I NOTICE?

Who's speaking, and what did they say?
Who's listening?

WHAT SHOULD I DO?

Do you see any bad examples? Who and why? Do you ever act like that bad example? Explain.

PRAYER:

Spend some time thinking about today's passage and write out a prayer to God. Ask Him to help you respond in the right way.

1 SAMUEL
BIG
IDEA

Outward appearances can be deceiving. God looks at the heart.

"He will protect his _____ ones, but the _____ will disappear in darkness. No one will succeed by _____ alone."

1 SAMUEL 2:9

WHAT DO I NOTICE?
What's repeated? Write down the repeated words or phrases and ask a parent or trusted Christian friend if you can circle them in your Bible!

WHAT SHOULD I DO?
Is there a verse that stands out? If so, which one, and why do you need to remember it?

PRAYER:
Spend some time thinking about today's passage and write out a prayer to God. Ask Him to help you respond in the right way.

_____

_____

_____

AUGUST
MEMORY
VERSE

"For even the Son of Man came not to be served but to serve others and to give his life as a ransom for many." – Mark 10:45

1 SAMUEL 4:2-11

"So the Philistines fought desperately, _____
_____
_____

1 SAMUEL 4:10

WHAT DO I NOTICE?

What's happening? Draw a picture or write 3 words that describe what you read!

WHAT SHOULD I DO?

Write down a truth about God you need to remember throughout your day.

PRAYER:

Spend some time thinking about today's passage and write out a prayer to God. Ask Him to help you respond in the right way.

_____
_____
_____

1 SAMUEL BIG IDEA

Outward appearances can be deceiving. God looks at the heart.

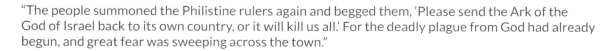

THURSDAY | GOD'S PRESENCE IS POWERFUL
1 SAMUEL 5:6-12

"The people summoned the Philistine rulers again and begged them, 'Please send the Ark of the God of Israel back to its own country, or it will kill us all.' For the deadly plague from God had already begun, and great fear was sweeping across the town."

1 SAMUEL 5:11

WHAT DO I NOTICE?
Where is this story taking place?
Ask a parent or trusted Christian friend to help you look it up on a map or in a Bible Atlas.

WHAT SHOULD I DO?
Write down a truth about God you need to remember throughout your day.

PRAYER:
Spend some time thinking about today's passage and write out a prayer to God. Ask Him to help you respond in the right way.

AUGUST
MEMORY
VERSE

"For even the Son of Man came not to be served but to serve others and to give his life as a ransom for many." – Mark 10:45

1 SAMUEL 7:1-15

"Then Samuel said to all the people of Israel, 'If you want to return to the Lord with all your hearts, get rid of your foreign _____ and your images of Ashtoreth. Turn your hearts to the Lord and _____ him _____; then he will rescue you from the Philistines.'"

1 SAMUEL 7:3

WHAT DO I NOTICE?
Who's speaking, and what did they say? Who's listening?

WHAT SHOULD I DO?
Do you see a good example? Is there an example to follow or instruction to obey? Explain.

PRAYER:
Spend some time thinking about today's passage and write out a prayer to God. Ask Him to help you respond in the right way.

_____

_____

_____

This week on the Journey Junior podcast we're talking about the Philistines and the Ark! Ask a parent or trusted Christian friend to help you listen to it!

LET'S PLAY A GAME

Can you fill in the blanks below and then help the Israelites
find the Ark of the Covenant in the maze?

"Put the Ark of the Lord on the _____, and beside it place a chest containing the gold _____ and gold tumors you are sending as a guilt _____. Then let the cows go wherever they want. If they cross the border of our land and go to Beth-shemesh, we will _____ it was the _____ who brought this great disaster upon us. If they don't, we will know it was not his hand that caused the plague. It came simply by _____.'" **1 SAMUEL 6:8-9**

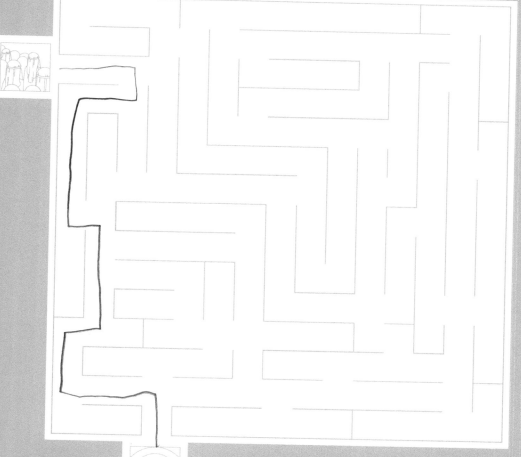

SUNDAY NOTES

1 SAMUEL 8:1-9

"'Do everything they say to you,' the Lord replied, 'for they are rejecting me, not you. They don't want me to be their king any longer.'"

1 SAMUEL 8:7

WHAT DO I NOTICE?

Who's speaking, and what do you know about them? Draw a picture of the speaker.

WHAT SHOULD I DO?

Do you see any bad examples? Who and why? Do you ever act like that bad example? Explain.

PRAYER:

Spend some time thinking about today's passage and write out a prayer to God. Ask Him to help you respond in the right way.

_____

_____

_____

1 SAMUEL
BIG
IDEA

Outward appearances can be deceiving. God looks at the heart.

"Saul replied, 'But I'm only from the tribe of _____, the smallest tribe in Israel, and my family is the least important of all the families of that tribe! Why are you talking like this to me?'"

1 SAMUEL 9:21

WHAT DO I NOTICE?
Where on the Bible Timeline does this story take place?

WHAT SHOULD I DO?
Write down a truth about God you need to remember throughout your day.

PRAYER:
Spend some time thinking about today's passage and write out a prayer to God. Ask Him to help you respond in the right way.

_____

_____

_____

AUGUST MEMORY VERSE

"For even the Son of Man came not to be served but to serve others and to give his life as a ransom for many." – Mark 10:45

1 SAMUEL 10:1-13

"At that time _____
_____
_____

1 SAMUEL 10:6

WHAT DO I NOTICE?

What's happening? Draw a picture or write 3 words that describe what you read!

WHAT SHOULD I DO?

Is there someone you need to share this truth with? Who will you tell, and what would you tell them?

PRAYER:

Spend some time thinking about today's passage and write out a prayer to God. Ask Him to help you respond in the right way.

_____
_____
_____

1 SAMUEL BIG IDEA

Outward appearances can be deceiving. God looks at the heart.

"But be sure to fear the Lord and faithfully serve him. Think of all the wonderful things he has done for you."

1 SAMUEL 12:24

WHAT DO I NOTICE?
Who's speaking, and what did they say? Who's listening?

WHAT SHOULD I DO?
Is there a verse that stands out? If so, which one, and why do you need to remember it?

PRAYER:
Spend some time thinking about today's passage and write out a prayer to God. Ask Him to help you respond in the right way.

AUGUST MEMORY VERSE

"For even the Son of Man came not to be served but to serve others and to give his life as a ransom for many." – Mark 10:45

33

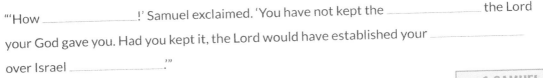

FRIDAY | DISOBEDIENCE IS FOOLISHNESS
1 SAMUEL 13:5-15

"'How _____!' Samuel exclaimed. 'You have not kept the _____ the Lord your God gave you. Had you kept it, the Lord would have established your _____ over Israel _____.'"

1 SAMUEL 13:13

WHAT DO I NOTICE?
What's happening? Draw a picture or write 3 words that describe what you read!

WHAT SHOULD I DO?
Do you see any bad examples? Who and why? Do you ever act like that bad example? Explain.

PRAYER:
Spend some time thinking about today's passage and write out a prayer to God. Ask Him to help you respond in the right way.

_____

_____

_____

Today on the Journey Junior podcast we're talking all about Saul being chosen as king! Make sure you tune in!

LET'S PLAY A GAME

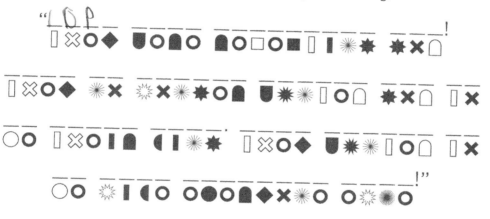

Why did the Israelites want Samuel to give them a king?

SUNDAY NOTES

1 SAMUEL 14:6-15

"'Let's go across to the outpost of those pagans,' Jonathan said to his armor bearer. 'Perhaps the Lord will help us, for nothing can hinder the Lord. He can win a battle whether he has many warriors or only a few!'"

1 SAMUEL 14:6

WHAT DO I NOTICE?

Where is this story taking place? Draw a picture of the setting.

WHAT SHOULD I DO?

Write down a truth about God you need to remember throughout your day.

PRAYER:

Spend some time thinking about today's passage and write out a prayer to God. Ask Him to help you respond in the right way.

1 SAMUEL BIG IDEA

Outward appearances can be deceiving. God looks at the heart.

TUESDAY | OBEY FULLY, NOT PARTIALLY
1 SAMUEL 15:1-3, 15:17-23

"But Samuel replied, 'What is more _____ to the Lord: your burnt offerings and sacrifices or your _____ to his voice? Listen! Obedience is _____ than sacrifice, and _____ is better than offering the fat of rams.'"

1 SAMUEL 15:22

WHAT DO I NOTICE?
Who's speaking, and what do you know about them? Draw a picture of the speaker.

WHAT SHOULD I DO?
Is there a verse that stands out? If so, which one, and why do you need to remember it?

PRAYER:
Spend some time thinking about today's passage and write out a prayer to God. Ask Him to help you respond in the right way.

_____

_____

_____

AUGUST MEMORY VERSE

"For even the Son of Man came not to be served but to serve others and to give his life as a ransom for many." – Mark 10:45

1 SAMUEL 16:1-13

"But the Lord said to Samuel, 'Don't judge by his appearance or height, for I have rejected him. The Lord doesn't see things the way you see them. People judge by outward appearance, but the Lord looks at the heart.'"

1 SAMUEL 16:7

WHAT DO I NOTICE?

What's happening? Draw a picture or write 3 words that describe what you read!

WHAT SHOULD I DO?

Write down a truth about God you need to remember throughout your day.

PRAYER:

Spend some time thinking about today's passage and write out a prayer to God. Ask Him to help you respond in the right way.

1 SAMUEL BIG IDEA

Outward appearances can be deceiving. God looks at the heart.

1 SAM. 17:3-11, 17:24-27, 17:36-50

"And everyone assembled here will know that the Lord rescues his people, but not with sword and spear. This is the Lord's battle, and he will give you to us!"

1 SAMUEL 17:47

WHAT DO I NOTICE?
What's happening? Draw a picture or write 3 words that describe what you read!

WHAT SHOULD I DO?
Do you see a good example? Is there an example to follow or instruction to obey? Explain.

PRAYER:
Spend some time thinking about today's passage and write out a prayer to God. Ask Him to help you respond in the right way.

AUGUST MEMORY VERSE

"For even the Son of Man came not to be served but to serve others and to give his life as a ransom for many." – Mark 10:45

"This made Saul very _____. 'What's this?' he said. 'They credit David with ten thousands and me with only thousands. Next they'll be making _____ their _____!'"

1 SAMUEL 18:8

WHAT DO I NOTICE?

What's repeated? Write down the repeated words or phrases and ask a parent or trusted Christian friend if you can circle them in your Bible!

WHAT SHOULD I DO?

Do you see any bad examples? Who and why? Do you ever act like that bad example? Explain.

PRAYER:

Spend some time thinking about today's passage and write out a prayer to God. Ask Him to help you respond in the right way.

_____

_____

_____

This week on the Join The Journey Jr. podcast we're exploring the story of David and Goliath!

TODAY'S DATE: _____

SUNDAY NOTES

_____
_____
_____
_____
_____
_____
_____
_____
_____
_____
_____
_____
_____
_____
_____
_____
_____
_____
_____

1 SAM. 20:12-22, 20:37-42

"So Jonathan made a solemn pact with David, saying, 'May the Lord destroy all your enemies!' And Jonathan made David reaffirm his vow of friendship again, for Jonathan loved David as he loved himself."

1 SAMUEL 20:16-17

WHAT DO I NOTICE?
Who's speaking, and what do you know about them? Draw a picture of the speaker.

WHAT SHOULD I DO?
Is there someone you need to share this truth with? Who will you tell, and what would you tell them?

PRAYER:
Spend some time thinking about today's passage and write out a prayer to God. Ask Him to help you respond in the right way.

1 SAMUEL BIG IDEA | Outward appearances can be deceiving. God looks at the heart.

"'This was certainly not the first time I had consulted God for him! May the king not accuse me and my family in this matter, for I knew nothing at all of any plot against you.' 'You will surely _____, Ahimelech, along with your entire _____!' the king shouted."

1 SAMUEL 22:15-16

WHAT DO I NOTICE?

Remember - the priests worked in the tabernacle (God's house). Inside the tabernacle was special bread that normal people weren't supposed to eat. In this instance, the priest makes a special exception to help David in his desperation.

What's happening? Draw a picture **or** write 3 words that describe what you read!

WHAT SHOULD I DO?

Sometimes, when people are upset, they do very unkind things. Whenever we read our Bibles, it is important that we remember we are reading stories about broken people. Sometimes we see these people make good choices, and other times we see them make bad choices. When they make bad choices, we can be encouraged by remembering that God doesn't give up on His children. God does not like those choices. He loves His children no matter what, but our bad choices make His heart sad. Whenever we see people treat others unfairly, we can be reminded that we serve a God of justice who will one day restore all things (Revelation 21:4)!

Do you see any bad examples? Who and why? Do you ever act like that bad example? Explain.

AUGUST MEMORY VERSE

"For even the Son of Man came not to be served but to serve others and to give his life as a ransom for many." – Mark 10:45

1 SAMUEL 23:1-5

"David asked the Lord, _____

_____

1 SAMUEL 23:2

WHAT DO I NOTICE?

Who's speaking, and what did they say? Who's listening?

WHAT SHOULD I DO?

Do you see a good example? Is there an example to follow or instruction to obey? Explain.

PRAYER:

Spend some time thinking about today's passage and write out a prayer to God. Ask Him to help you respond in the right way.

_____

_____

_____

1 SAMUEL BIG IDEA

Outward appearances can be deceiving. God looks at the heart.

1 SAMUEL 24:3-12, 24:16-20

"And he said to David, 'You are a better man than I am, for you have repaid me good for evil.'"

1 SAMUEL 24:17

WHAT DO I NOTICE?
What's happening? Draw a picture or write 3 words that describe what you read!

WHAT SHOULD I DO?
Is there a verse that stands out? If so, which one, and why do you need to remember it?

PRAYER:
Spend some time thinking about today's passage and write out a prayer to God. Ask Him to help you respond in the right way.

_____

_____

_____

AUGUST MEMORY VERSE | "For even the Son of Man came not to be served but to serve others and to give his life as a ransom for many." – Mark 10:45

FRIDAY | GOOD SENSE DOES GOD'S WILL, NOT OURS
1 SAM. 25:9-22, 25:32-35

"Thank God for your good sense! Bless you for keeping me from _____ and from carrying out vengeance with my _____ hands."

1 SAMUEL 25:33

WHAT DO I NOTICE?
What's happening? Draw a picture or write 3 words that describe what you read!

WHAT SHOULD I DO?
Do you see a good example? Is there an example to follow or instruction to obey? Explain.

PRAYER:
Spend some time thinking about today's passage and write out a prayer to God. Ask Him to help you respond in the right way.

_____

_____

_____

Jonathan showed just how good of a friend he was to David by warning him. We're talking all about this friendship on today's podcast.

LET'S PLAY A GAME

One day after Samuel had come by to anoint David, he found himself standing around with some of his brothers (they were probably being super nice to their future king)! Each brother is represented by a shape.

Eliab   Abinadad   Shammah   Nethanel   David

Can you put them in order of how they're standing based on these clues? Use the empty boxes below to fill in their names!

CLUES:
- David is standing next to Eliab.
- Shammah is somewhere to the right of Nethanel.
- Eliab is in the spot second from the right.
- Nethanel is standing next to David.
- Abinadad is next to Nethanel.

TODAY'S DATE: _____

SUNDAY NOTES

1 SAMUEL 26:1-14, 26:17-18, 26:21-22

"'No!' David said. 'Don't kill him. For who can remain innocent after attacking the Lord's anointed one? Surely the Lord will strike Saul down someday, or he will die of old age or in battle.'"

1 SAMUEL 26:9-10

WHAT DO I NOTICE?

Who's speaking, and what do you know about them? Draw a picture of the speaker.

WHAT SHOULD I DO?

Write down a truth about God you need to remember throughout your day.

PRAYER:

Spend some time thinking about today's passage and write out a prayer to God. Ask Him to help you respond in the right way.

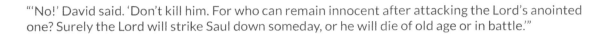

1 SAMUEL BIG IDEA | Outward appearances can be deceiving. God looks at the heart.

"But David kept thinking to himself, 'Someday Saul is going to get me. The best thing I can do is _____ to the Philistines. Then Saul will stop _____ for me in Israelite territory, and I will finally be _____.'"

1 SAMUEL 27:1

WHAT DO I NOTICE?
What's happening? Draw a picture or write 3 words that describe what you read!

WHAT SHOULD I DO?
Do you see any bad examples? Who and why? Do you ever act like that bad example? Explain.

PRAYER:
Spend some time thinking about today's passage and write out a prayer to God. Ask Him to help you respond in the right way.

_____

_____

_____

AUGUST MEMORY VERSE

"For even the Son of Man came not to be served but to serve others and to give his life as a ransom for many." – Mark 10:45

1 SAMUEL 29:1-11

"But Achish insisted, 'As far as I'm concerned, you're as perfect as an angel of God. _____

_____

1 SAMUEL 29:9

WHAT DO I NOTICE?

Who's speaking, and what did they say?
Who's listening?

WHAT SHOULD I DO?

Is there a verse that stands out? If so,
which one, and why do you need to
remember it?

PRAYER:

Spend some time thinking about today's passage and write out a prayer to God. Ask Him to help
you respond in the right way.

_____

_____

_____

1 SAMUEL
BIG
IDEA

Outward appearances can be deceiving. God looks at the heart.

1 SAMUEL 30:1-20

"Then David asked the Lord, 'Should I chase after this band of raiders? Will I catch them?' And the Lord told him, 'Yes, go after them. You will surely recover everything that was taken from you!'"

1 SAMUEL 30:8

WHAT DO I NOTICE?

What's happening? Draw a picture or write 3 words that describe what you read!

WHAT SHOULD I DO?

Do you see a good example? Is there an example to follow or instruction to obey? Explain.

PRAYER:

Spend some time thinking about today's passage and write out a prayer to God. Ask Him to help you respond in the right way.

AUGUST
MEMORY
VERSE

"For even the Son of Man came not to be served but to serve others and to give his life as a ransom for many." – Mark 10:45

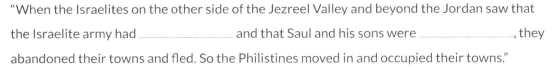

"When the Israelites on the other side of the Jezreel Valley and beyond the Jordan saw that the Israelite army had _____ and that Saul and his sons were _____, they abandoned their towns and fled. So the Philistines moved in and occupied their towns."

1 SAMUEL 31:7

WHAT DO I NOTICE?

What's happening? Draw a picture or write 3 words that describe what you read!

PRAYER:

Spend some time thinking about today's passage and write out a prayer to God. Ask Him to help you respond in the right way.

_____

_____

_____

WHAT SHOULD I DO?

Sometimes, when people make bad choices, they will do anything to escape the consequences of their actions. Just as Adam and Eve hid from God in the garden (or we push toys under our beds when we are supposed to have cleaned our rooms), Saul uses death to try to escape the consequences of his choices. But hiding and death are NEVER the answer. Whenever we are afraid of the consequences that might result from a bad choice, we should always bring them into the light. Secrets can act like poison in our hearts, but the Bible tells us that there is safety when we are honest (Proverbs 10:9). If you've made a poor choice that you've kept secret, take a step of courage and tell a parent or trusted Christian friend. Ask them for their forgiveness and to pray for you.

Do you see any bad examples? Who and why? Do you ever act like that bad example? Explain.

Today on the podcast: David spares Saul!

TODAY'S DATE: _____

SUNDAY NOTES

_____

_____

_____

_____

_____

_____

_____

_____

_____

_____

_____

_____

_____

_____

_____

_____

_____

_____

_____

_____

_____

2 SAMUEL

 No one is immune to sin.

HELPFUL HINTS:

- **Sin** – Anything we think, say, or do that does not please or honor God
- **God is faithful** – He always keeps His promises
- **Idol** – Anything we make more important than God

2 SAMUEL

MONDAY | LOVE THOSE WHO HURT YOU
2 SAMUEL 1:1-12

"They mourned and wept and fasted all day for Saul and his son Jonathan, and for the Lord's army and the nation of Israel, because they had died by the sword that day."

2 SAMUEL 1:12

WHAT DO I NOTICE?
Who's speaking, and what did they say?
Who's listening?

WHAT SHOULD I DO?
Is there a verse that stands out? If so, which one, and why do you need to remember it?

PRAYER:
Spend some time thinking about today's passage and write out a prayer to God. Ask Him to help you respond in the right way.

_____

_____

_____

2 SAMUEL
BIG
IDEA

No one is immune to sin.

2 SAMUEL 2:1-11, 3:1, 3:17-19

"That was the beginning of a long _____ between those who were _____ to Saul and those _____ to David. As time passed David became _____ and stronger, while Saul's dynasty became _____ and weaker."

2 SAMUEL 3:1

WHAT DO I NOTICE?
Who's speaking, and what do you know about them? Draw a picture of the speaker.

WHAT SHOULD I DO?
Is there a promise you need to remember? If so, what is it?

PRAYER:
Spend some time thinking about today's passage and write out a prayer to God. Ask Him to help you respond in the right way.

_____

_____

_____

"In the same way, let your good deeds shine out for all to see, so that everyone will praise your heavenly Father." – Matthew 5:16

2 SAMUEL 4:1-11

"They went into the house and found Ishbosheth sleeping on his bed. They struck and killed him and cut off his head. Then, taking his head with them, they fled across the Jordan Valley through the night. When they arrived at Hebron, they presented Ishbosheth's head to David. 'Look!' they exclaimed to the king. 'Here is the head of Ishbosheth, the son of your enemy Saul who tried to kill you. Today the Lord has given my lord the king revenge on Saul and his entire family!'"

2 SAMUEL 4:7-8

WHAT DO I NOTICE?

Sometimes, out of anger, people make bad choices. These choices make God's heart very sad. Whenever we see people making bad choices in the Bible, it's important for us to take note of how both God and the people of God respond to them.

What's happening? Draw a picture or write 3 words that describe what you read!

WHAT SHOULD I DO?

Do you see any bad examples? Who and why? Do you ever act like that bad example? Explain.

PRAYER:

Spend some time thinking about today's passage and write out a prayer to God. Ask Him to help you respond in the right way.

_____

_____

_____

2 SAMUEL BIG IDEA

No one is immune to sin.

"And David became more and more powerful, because the Lord God of Heaven's Armies was with him."

2 SAMUEL 5:10

WHAT DO I NOTICE?

Where on the Bible Timeline does this story take place?

WHAT SHOULD I DO?

Is there someone you need to share this truth with? Who will you tell, and what would you tell them?

PRAYER:

Spend some time thinking about today's passage and write out a prayer to God. Ask Him to help you respond in the right way.

_____

_____

_____

"In the same way, let your good deeds shine out for all to see, so that everyone will praise your heavenly Father." – Matthew 5:16

FRIDAY | ASK BEFORE YOU ACT
2 SAMUEL 6:1-15

"But when they arrived at the threshing floor of Nacon, the oxen stumbled, and Uzzah reached out his hand and steadied the Ark of God. Then the Lord's _____ was aroused against Uzzah, and God struck him _____ because of this. So Uzzah died right there beside the Ark of God."

2 SAMUEL 6:6-7

WHAT DO I NOTICE?

The Ark of the Covenant was a box or chest that God told the Israelites to make as a sign of His promises to them. The lid of the Ark was called the "Mercy Seat." Once a year, a priest would sprinkle the blood of an animal on the seat to make payment (atone) for the sins of Israel. The Ark was very, very special and needed to be handled with great and specific care.

How did the people respond to God? How did God respond to the people?

WHAT SHOULD I DO?

Do you see any bad examples? Who and why? Do you ever act like that bad example? Explain.

PRAYER:

Spend some time thinking about today's passage and write out a prayer to God. Ask Him to help you respond in the right way.

Today on the Join The Journey Jr. podcast we're exploring David being anointed as king!

TODAY'S DATE: _____

SUNDAY NOTES

_____
_____
_____
_____
_____
_____
_____
_____
_____
_____
_____
_____
_____
_____
_____
_____
_____
_____

2 SAMUEL 7:1-17

"For when you die and are buried with your ancestors, I will raise up one of your descendants, your own offspring, and I will make his kingdom strong."

2 SAMUEL 7:12

WHAT DO I NOTICE?

2 Samuel 7 is one of the most noteworthy passages in the Old Testament. In verses 13-15, God makes some very important promises to David and his family. God promised David He would build his family into a great house. Someone from his family would always rule. One day, God would bring the perfect king forever, the Messiah.

Who's speaking, and what did they say? Who's listening?

WHAT SHOULD I DO?

Is there a verse that stands out? If so, which one, and why do you need to remember it?

PRAYER:

Spend some time thinking about today's passage and write out a prayer to God. Ask Him to help you respond in the right way.

2 SAMUEL
BIG
IDEA

No one is immune to sin.

2 SAMUEL 9:1-13

"'Don't be afraid!' David said. 'I intend to show _____ to you because of my promise to your father, Jonathan. I will give you all the _____ that once belonged to your grandfather Saul, and you will _____ here with me at the king's table!'"

2 SAMUEL 9:7

WHAT DO I NOTICE?

What's happening? Draw a picture or write 3 words that describe what you read!

WHAT SHOULD I DO?

Do you see a good example? Is there an example to follow or instruction to obey? Explain.

PRAYER:

Spend some time thinking about today's passage and write out a prayer to God. Ask Him to help you respond in the right way.

_____

_____

_____

SEPTEMBER MEMORY VERSE

"In the same way, let your good deeds shine out for all to see, so that everyone will praise your heavenly Father." – Matthew 5:16

2 SAMUEL 10:9-19

"Be courageous! _____

_____

2 SAMUEL 10:12

WHAT DO I NOTICE?

What's happening? Draw a picture or write 3 words that describe what you read!

WHAT SHOULD I DO?

Do you see any bad examples? Who and why? Do you ever act like that bad example? Explain.

PRAYER:

Spend some time thinking about today's passage and write out a prayer to God. Ask Him to help you respond in the right way.

_____

_____

_____

2 SAMUEL
BIG
IDEA

No one is immune to sin.

"Why, then, have you despised the word of the Lord and done this horrible deed? For you have murdered Uriah the Hittite with the sword of the Ammonites and stolen his wife."

2 SAMUEL 12:9

WHAT DO I NOTICE?
Who's speaking, and what did they say? Who's listening?

WHAT SHOULD I DO?
Do you see any bad examples? Who and why? Do you ever act like that bad example? Explain.

PRAYER:
Spend some time thinking about today's passage and write out a prayer to God. Ask Him to help you respond in the right way.

SEPTEMBER MEMORY VERSE

"In the same way, let your good deeds shine out for all to see, so that everyone will praise your heavenly Father." – Matthew 5:16

"But God does not just _____ life away; instead, he devises ways to bring us

_____ when we have been _____ from _____."

2 SAMUEL 14:14B

WHAT DO I NOTICE?

Who's speaking, and what do you know about them? Draw a picture of the speaker.

WHAT SHOULD I DO?

Is there a verse that stands out? If so, which one, and why do you need to remember it?

PRAYER:

Spend some time thinking about today's passage and write out a prayer to God. Ask Him to help you respond in the right way.

_____

_____

_____

What is the Davidic Covenant? We're talking all about God's promises to David on today's episode of the Join The Journey Jr. podcast.

LET'S PLAY A GAME

What Did God Promise David?

"___ ___ ___ ___ ___ ___ ___ ___ ___ ___
6 15 18 23 8 5 14 25 15 21 4 9 5 1 14 4 1 18 5 2 21 18 9 5 4

___ ___ ___ ___ ___ ___, ___ ___ ___ ___
23 9 20 8 25 15 21 18 1 14 3 5 19 20 15 18 19, 9 23 9 12 12 18 1 9 19 5

___ ___ ___ ___ ___ ___, ___
21 16 15 14 5 15 6 25 15 21 18 4 5 19 3 5 14 4 1 14 20 19, 25 15 21 18

___ ___ ___, ___ ___ ___ ___
15 23 14 15 6 6 19 16 18 9 14 7, 1 14 4 9 23 9 12 12 13 1 11 5

___ ___ ___ ___. ___ ___ ___ ___
8 9 19 11 9 14 7 4 15 13 19 20 18 15 14 7. 8 5 9 19 20 8 5 15 14 5

___ ___ ___ ___ ___ ___ ___
23 8 15 23 9 12 12 2 21 9 12 4 1 8 15 21 19 5 1 20 5 13 16 12 5

___ ___ ___. ___ ___ ___ ___ ___
6 15 18 13 25 14 1 13 5. 1 14 4 9 23 9 12 12 19 5 3 21 18 5 8 9 19

___ ___ ___."
18 15 25 1 12 20 8 18 15 14 5 6 15 18 5 22 5 18."

A — 1	E — 5	I — 9	M — 13	Q — 17	U — 21	Y — 25
B — 2	F — 6	J — 10	N — 14	R — 18	V — 22	Z — 26
C — 3	G — 7	K — 11	O — 15	S — 19	W — 23	
D — 4	H — 8	L — 12	P — 16	T — 20	X — 24	

SUNDAY NOTES

2 SAMUEL 16:11-19, 17:5-18

"Then Absalom and all the men of Israel said, 'Hushai's advice is better than Ahithophel's.' For the Lord had determined to defeat the counsel of Ahithophel, which really was the better plan, so that he could bring disaster on Absalom!"

2 SAMUEL 17:14

WHAT DO I NOTICE?

Absalom is David's son. Absalom made choices that went against God's best. He ran away because he was scared his father would be angry. While he was away, he decided that he wanted to be the next king of Israel. He was willing to do whatever it took to be king. Ultimately, God allowed Absalom to face the consequences of his sins.

What's happening? Draw a picture or write 3 words that describe what you read!

WHAT SHOULD I DO?

Do you see any bad examples? Who and why? Do you ever act like that bad example? Explain.

PRAYER:

Spend some time thinking about today's passage and write out a prayer to God. Ask Him to help you respond in the right way.

2 SAMUEL BIG IDEA

No one is immune to sin.

2 SAM. 18:19-22, 18:33, 19:14-23

"Then Amasa convinced all the men of Judah, and they responded unanimously. They sent word to the king, '_____ to us, and bring _____ all who are with you.'"

2 SAMUEL 19:14

WHAT DO I NOTICE?
What's happening? Draw a picture or write 3 words that describe what you read!

WHAT SHOULD I DO?
Is there a verse that stands out? If so, which one, and why do you need to remember it?

PRAYER:
Spend some time thinking about today's passage and write out a prayer to God. Ask Him to help you respond in the right way.

_____

_____

_____

"In the same way, let your good deeds shine out for all to see, so that everyone will praise your heavenly Father." – Matthew 5:16

2 SAMUEL 20:1-2, 20:16-23

"I'm one who is peace loving and faithful in Israel. _____

_____

_____

2 SAMUEL 20:19

WHAT DO I NOTICE?

Who's speaking, and what did they say?
Who's listening?

WHAT SHOULD I DO?

Is there someone you need to share this truth with? Who will you tell, and what would you tell them?

PRAYER:

Spend some time thinking about today's passage and write out a prayer to God. Ask Him to help you respond in the right way.

_____

_____

_____

2 SAMUEL
BIG
IDEA

No one is immune to sin.

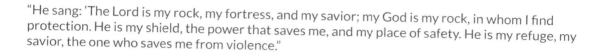

"He sang: 'The Lord is my rock, my fortress, and my savior; my God is my rock, in whom I find protection. He is my shield, the power that saves me, and my place of safety. He is my refuge, my savior, the one who saves me from violence."

2 SAMUEL 22:2-3

WHAT DO I NOTICE?
What's repeated? Write down the repeated words or phrases and ask a parent or trusted Christian friend if you can circle them in your Bible!

WHAT SHOULD I DO?
Write down a truth about God you need to remember throughout your day.

PRAYER:
Spend some time thinking about today's passage and write out a prayer to God. Ask Him to help you respond in the right way.

SEPTEMBER MEMORY VERSE

"In the same way, let your good deeds shine out for all to see, so that everyone will praise your heavenly Father." – Matthew 5:16

"But after he had taken the _____, David's conscience began to bother him. And he said to the Lord, 'I have sinned greatly by taking this census. Please forgive my _____, Lord, for doing this _____ thing.'"

2 SAMUEL 24:10

WHAT DO I NOTICE?

Towards the end of David's life, he decided to take a census, or count how many people there were. He wanted to know how many men could fight in a battle. Counting people is not wrong. The reason David wanted to count the men was that he didn't trust that God would provide what the people of Israel needed in battle. David's heart was the problem, and that was why God punished David.

How did the people respond to God? How did God respond to the people?

WHAT SHOULD I DO?

Do you see a good example? Is there an example to follow or instruction to obey? Explain.

PRAYER:

Spend some time thinking about today's passage and write out a prayer to God. Ask Him to help you respond in the right way.

_____

_____

_____

Today on the Join The Journey Jr. podcast, we're doing a recap on the life of King David!

LET'S PLAY A GAME

Where were the 12 tribes supposed to live?

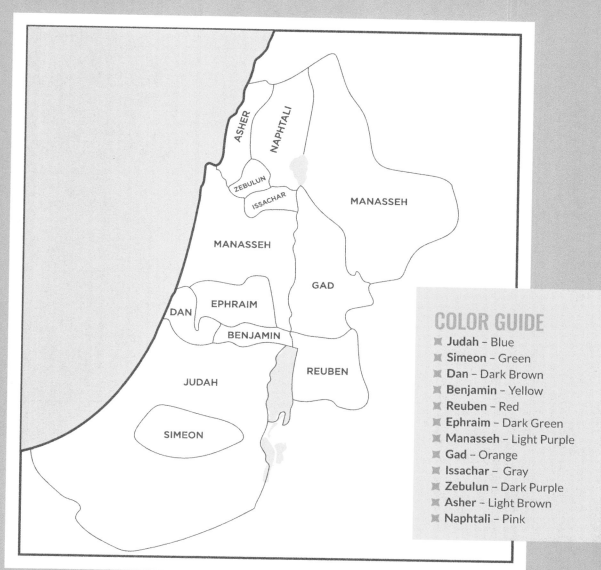

COLOR GUIDE

- **Judah** – Blue
- **Simeon** – Green
- **Dan** – Dark Brown
- **Benjamin** – Yellow
- **Reuben** – Red
- **Ephraim** – Dark Green
- **Manasseh** – Light Purple
- **Gad** – Orange
- **Issachar** – Gray
- **Zebulun** – Dark Purple
- **Asher** – Light Brown
- **Naphtali** – Pink

SUNDAY NOTES

1 KINGS

 Wise leaders walk closely with God.

HELPFUL HINTS:

- **God** – The all-powerful, all-knowing, all-seeing Creator of everything
- **Bible** – The written Word of God
- **Glory** – God's perfect goodness and greatness
- **Glorify** – Pointing to or reflecting God's glory

1 KINGS

1 KINGS 1:28-37

"And the king repeated his vow: 'As surely as the Lord lives, who has rescued me from every danger, your son Solomon will be the next king and will sit on my throne this very day, just as I vowed to you before the Lord, the God of Israel.'"

1 KINGS 1:29-30

WHAT DO I NOTICE?

Who's speaking, and what do you know about them? Draw a picture of the speaker.

WHAT SHOULD I DO?

Is there a verse that stands out? If so, which one, and why do you need to remember it?

PRAYER:

Spend some time thinking about today's passage and write out a prayer to God. Ask Him to help you respond in the right way.

1 KINGS
BIG
IDEA

Wise leaders walk closely with God.

"Solomon became _____ and sat on the _____ of David his father, and his kingdom was _____ established."

1 KINGS 2:12

WHAT DO I NOTICE?
Who's speaking, and what did they say? Who's listening?

Where on the Bible Timeline does this story take place?

WHAT SHOULD I DO?
Is there instruction you can apply to your own life? If so, what are the instructions?

PRAYER:
Spend some time thinking about today's passage and write out a prayer to God. Ask Him to help you respond in the right way.

_____

_____

_____

SEPTEMBER MEMORY VERSE

"In the same way, let your good deeds shine out for all to see, so that everyone will praise your heavenly Father." – Matthew 5:16

1 KINGS 3:5-15

"Give me an understanding heart so that I can govern your people well _____
_____
_____

1 KINGS 3:9

WHAT DO I NOTICE?

Who's speaking, and what did they say?
Who's listening?

WHAT SHOULD I DO?

Do you see a good example? Is there an example to follow or instruction to obey? Explain.

PRAYER:

Spend some time thinking about today's passage and write out a prayer to God. Ask Him to help you respond in the right way.

_____
_____
_____

1 KINGS
BIG
IDEA

Wise leaders walk closely with God.

"And kings from every nation sent their ambassadors to listen to the wisdom of Solomon."

1 KINGS 4:34

WHAT DO I NOTICE?

Where is this story taking place?
Ask a parent or trusted Christian friend to help you look it up on a map or in a Bible Atlas.

WHAT SHOULD I DO?

Is there a verse that stands out? If so, which one, and why do you need to remember it?

PRAYER:

Spend some time thinking about today's passage and write out a prayer to God. Ask Him to help you respond in the right way.

SEPTEMBER
MEMORY
VERSE

"In the same way, let your good deeds shine out for all to see,
so that everyone will praise your heavenly Father." – Matthew 5:16

87

1 KINGS 5:1-12

"So I am planning to build a _____ to _____ the name of the Lord my God, just as he had instructed my father, David. For the Lord told him, 'Your _____, whom I will place on your _____, will build the Temple to honor my name.'"

1 KINGS 5:5

WHAT DO I NOTICE?

Remember back in the book of Numbers when the Israelites would pack up the tabernacle (God's tent) and take it with them as they traveled? Now, thanks to Solomon's leadership, the tabernacle was getting an upgrade! It was no longer going to be a tent. Instead, it was a magnificent structure! Think about the temple as the permanent place for people to worship God. It was where priests would sacrifice animals and make offerings to God.

What's happening? Draw a picture or write 3 words that describe what you read!

WHAT SHOULD I DO?

Do you see a good example? Is there an example to follow or instruction to obey? Explain.

PRAYER:

Spend some time thinking about today's passage and write out a prayer to God. Ask Him to help you respond in the right way.

Today on the Journey Jr. podcast, we're talking all about Solomon's wisdom!

LET'S PLAY A GAME

```
B P R A Y E R R S W T U M X L
A X T U N M T V R I C H E S E
S O L O M O N D S S T X V W L
M P T A B G E R T D L N E T U
A C K G O O D G N O P T F M F
R W R Y I P S F Q M M O A B H
T I N S P V L Q N C W A I X C
Y L E A D E R S H I P D T A N
P H F A M O U S T Q P U H R S
E V M N D V L K M K Q E F F I
V C P R A A F A V O R F U C N
I P T X V T B H B J K N L M L
L C R U I H M H S R S P T Q L
N E U N D E R S T A N D I N G
L C M W U E Q P S F P M H G Z
```

SOLOMON	LEADERSHIP	FAMOUS
WISDOM	RICHES	UNDERSTANDING
PRAYER	SMART	GOOD
DAVID	FAVOR	EVIL
SIN	FAITHFUL	

89

TODAY'S DATE: _____

SUNDAY NOTES

1 KINGS 6:11-22

"I will live among the Israelites and will never abandon my people Israel."

WHAT DO I NOTICE?

The temple was made up of two primary parts: The Holy Place and the Most Holy Place (sometimes it's called the Holy of Holies). The Most Holy Place is where the Ark of the Covenant was kept. These two rooms were separated by a veil (think along the lines of a very fancy shower curtain)! Once a year, the priests would go into the Most Holy Place on the Day of Atonement to make an offering that would cover the sins of the people.

Where is this story taking place? Draw a picture of the setting.

WHAT SHOULD I DO?

God cared about the details of the tabernacle! Of course, God was worthy of the very best temple His people could build. Solomon wanted to offer God the best of the best.

Do you offer God your very best? Explain.

PRAYER:

Spend some time thinking about today's passage and write out a prayer to God. Ask Him to help you respond in the right way.

_____

_____

_____

Wise leaders walk closely with God.

TUESDAY | GOD IS WORTHY OF OUR WORSHIP
1 KINGS 7:45-51

"So King Solomon _____ all his work on the Temple of the Lord. Then he brought all the _____ his father, David, had dedicated—the silver, the _____, and the various articles—and he stored them in the _____ of the Lord's Temple."

1 KINGS 7:51

WHAT DO I NOTICE?
What's repeated? How many times does the repeated word or phrase appear in this passage?

PRAYER:
Spend some time thinking about today's passage and write out a prayer to God. Ask Him to help you respond in the right way.

WHAT SHOULD I DO?
When we think about the items in the temple, we can see how they all point to Jesus! For example, the Table of Showbread represented God spiritually sustaining the Israelites when they wandered in the desert. Jesus tells us that He is the bread of life! He spiritually sustains believers every day. In the Old Testament, God's people were required to do many things to follow the law, though they could never perfectly keep the law. They would do many of these things in the temple. When Jesus came, He met all of the requirements, or high standards, of the law. Now, we no longer have to follow these rules and regulations in order to have a good (right) relationship with God.

Write down a truth about God you need to remember throughout your day.

"Trust in the Lord with all your heart; do not depend on your own understanding. Seek his will in all you do, and he will show you which path to take." – Proverbs 3:5-6

1 KINGS 8:1-11

"When the priests came out of the Holy Place, _____

_____

_____

1 KINGS 8:10-11

WHAT DO I NOTICE?

What's happening? Draw a picture or write 3 words that describe what you read!

WHAT SHOULD I DO?

Is there a verse that stands out? If so, which one, and why do you need to remember it?

PRAYER:

Spend some time thinking about today's passage and write out a prayer to God. Ask Him to help you respond in the right way.

_____

_____

_____

1 KINGS
BIG
IDEA

Wise leaders walk closely with God.

1 KINGS 9:1-9

"But if you or your descendants abandon me and disobey the commands and decrees I have given you, and if you serve and worship other gods, then I will uproot Israel from this land that I have given them. I will reject this Temple that I have made holy to honor my name. I will make Israel an object of mockery and ridicule among the nations."

1 KINGS 9:6-7

WHAT DO I NOTICE?

Who's speaking, and what did they say? Who's listening?

WHAT SHOULD I DO?

Do you see a good example? Is there an example to follow or instruction to obey? Explain.

PRAYER:

Spend some time thinking about today's passage and write out a prayer to God. Ask Him to help you respond in the right way.

OCTOBER MEMORY VERSE

"Trust in the Lord with all your heart; do not depend on your own understanding. Seek his will in all you do, and he will show you which path to take." – Proverbs 3:5-6

1 KINGS 10:1-10

"Praise the Lord your God, who _____ in you and has placed you on the throne of Israel. Because of the Lord's eternal _____ for Israel, he has made you _____ so you can rule with _____ and _____."

1 KINGS 10:9

WHAT DO I NOTICE?

Who's speaking, and what do you know about them? Draw a picture of the speaker.

WHAT SHOULD I DO?

Write down a truth about God you need to remember throughout your day.

PRAYER:

Spend some time thinking about today's passage and write out a prayer to God. Ask Him to help you respond in the right way.

_____

_____

_____

Today on the Journey Jr. podcast, we're talking all about God's glory!

TODAY'S DATE: _____

SUNDAY NOTES

97

1 KINGS 11:1-13

"In this way, Solomon did what was evil in the Lord's sight; he refused to follow the Lord completely, as his father, David, had done."

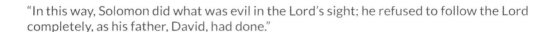

1 KINGS 11:6

WHAT DO I NOTICE?

Look at verses 11-13. These verses show us the consequence that resulted from Solomon's sin.

What was Solomon's consequence?

WHAT SHOULD I DO?

Do you see any bad examples? Who and why? Do you ever act like that bad example? Explain.

PRAYER:

Spend some time thinking about today's passage and write out a prayer to God. Ask Him to help you respond in the right way.

1 KINGS
BIG
IDEA

Wise leaders walk closely with God.

"Yes, my father laid _____ burdens on you, but I'm going to make them even

_____! My father beat you with whips, but I will beat you with _____!"

1 KINGS 12:11

WHAT DO I NOTICE?
Solomon's son was named Rehoboam. Remember, God said that Solomon's sin would affect the kingdom when his son was in charge...

What happened with Rehoboam?

WHAT SHOULD I DO?
Do you see any bad examples? Who and why? Do you ever act like that bad example? Explain.

PRAYER:
Spend some time thinking about today's passage and write out a prayer to God. Ask Him to help you respond in the right way.

_____

_____

_____

"Trust in the Lord with all your heart; do not depend on your own understanding. Seek his will in all you do, and he will show you which path to take." – Proverbs 3:5-6

1 KINGS 12:25-33

"But this became a great sin, _____

_____

1 KINGS 12:30

WHAT DO I NOTICE?

*Jeroboam was a servant of the king. Sometimes, it can be easy for us to accidentally mix up Rehoboam and Jeroboam. Think about it like this - Rehoboam had the **RIGHT** to rule the kingdom; Jeroboam didn't.*

What's happening? Draw a picture or write 3 words that describe what you read!

WHAT SHOULD I DO?

Do you see any bad examples? Who and why? Do you ever act like that bad example? Explain.

PRAYER:

Spend some time thinking about today's passage and write out a prayer to God. Ask Him to help you respond in the right way.

_____

_____

_____

1 KINGS BIG IDEA

Wise leaders walk closely with God.

1 KINGS 14:1-17

"In addition, the Lord will raise up a king over Israel who will destroy the family of Jeroboam. This will happen today, even now! ... He will abandon Israel because Jeroboam sinned and made Israel sin along with him."

1 KINGS 14:14,16

WHAT SHOULD I DO?

1 Kings 14 is a hard story to read. It's OK to be sad about what happened to Jeroboam's son and to ask questions about it. Remember, we live in a broken world. Sin has touched everything around us. There are always consequences for sin. Sometimes, our sin impacts others even if they don't deserve it. We know that God is all-powerful and just. He is in control of everything and cannot let sin go unpunished. God did not cause this to happen to Jeroboam's son, but He allowed it to happen. God is loving, and He loves Jeroboam's son very much. The good news is, we can look forward to the day when all of the bad things in our world will go away forever!

What's happening? Draw a picture or write 3 words that describe what you read!

WHAT DO I NOTICE?

Do you see any bad examples? Who and why? Do you ever act like that bad example? Explain.

PRAYER:

Spend some time thinking about today's passage and write out a prayer to God. Ask Him to help you respond in the right way.

_____

_____

_____

OCTOBER
MEMORY
VERSE

"Trust in the Lord with all your heart; do not depend on your own understanding. Seek his will in all you do, and he will show you which path to take." – Proverbs 3:5-6

"But Ahab son of Omri did what was _____ in the Lord's sight, even _____

than any of the _____ before him."

1 KINGS 16:30

WHAT DO I NOTICE?

Remember what God said would happen because of Solomon's sin? God kept his word, and the kingdom of Israel was divided into two smaller kingdoms. The northern kingdom kept the name Israel, while the smaller southern kingdom was called Judah.

Where is this story taking place? Ask a parent or trusted Christian friend to help you look it up on a map or in a Bible Atlas.

WHAT SHOULD I DO?

Omri and Ahab did not make good choices. They did not trust in God and obey His commandments.

What should they have done instead? If you were in their shoes, what do you think you would have done?

PRAYER:

Spend some time thinking about today's passage and write out a prayer to God. Ask Him to help you respond in the right way.

_____

_____

Disobeying God and following our own way leads to destruction - check out today's podcast with a parent or trusted Christian friend!

LET'S PLAY A GAME

What did God say to Solomon after he disobeyed?

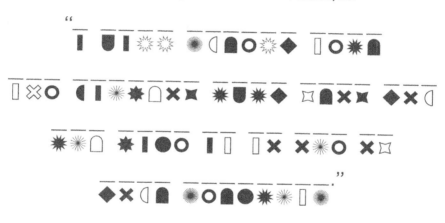

SUNDAY NOTES

1 KINGS 17:1-24

"The Lord heard Elijah's prayer, and the life of the child returned, and he revived!"

1 KINGS 17:22

WHAT DO I NOTICE?
Who's speaking, and what did they say? Who's listening?

WHAT SHOULD I DO?
Do you see a good example? Is there an example to follow or instruction to obey? Explain.

PRAYER:
Spend some time thinking about today's passage and write out a prayer to God. Ask Him to help you respond in the right way.

---

1 KINGS BIG IDEA | Wise leaders walk closely with God.

1 KINGS 18:1-19

"But Elijah said, 'I swear by the Lord Almighty, in whose presence I _____, that I will _____ myself to _____ this very day.'"

1 KINGS 18:15

WHAT DO I NOTICE?
What's happening? Draw a picture or write 3 words that describe what you read!

WHAT SHOULD I DO?
Do you see any bad examples? Who and why? Do you ever act like that bad example? Explain.

PRAYER:
Spend some time thinking about today's passage and write out a prayer to God. Ask Him to help you respond in the right way.

_____

_____

_____

OCTOBER
MEMORY
VERSE

"Trust in the Lord with all your heart; do not depend on your own understanding. Seek his will in all you do, and he will show you which path to take." – Proverbs 3:5-6

1 KINGS 18:20-40

"Immediately the fire of the Lord flashed down from heaven and burned up the young bull, the wood, the stones, and the dust. It even licked up all the water in the trench! And when all the people saw it, they fell face down on the ground and cried out, 'The Lord—he is God! Yes, the Lord is God!'"

1 KINGS 18:38-39

WHAT DO I NOTICE?

How did the people respond to God?
How did God respond to the people?

WHAT SHOULD I DO?

Write down a truth about God you need to remember throughout your day.

PRAYER:

Spend some time thinking about today's passage and write out a prayer to God. Ask Him to help you respond in the right way.

_____

_____

_____

1 KINGS BIG IDEA | Wise leaders walk closely with God.

1 KINGS 19:1-21

"And after the earthquake there was a fire, but the Lord was not in the fire. And after the fire there was the sound of a gentle whisper."

1 KINGS 19:12

WHAT DO I NOTICE?

Who's speaking, and what did they say? Who's listening?

WHAT SHOULD I DO?

Is there someone you need to share this truth with? Who will you tell, and what would you tell them?

PRAYER:

Spend some time thinking about today's passage and write out a prayer to God. Ask Him to help you respond in the right way.

"Trust in the Lord with all your heart; do not depend on your own understanding. Seek his will in all you do, and he will show you which path to take." – Proverbs 3:5-6

1 KINGS 20:35-43

"The prophet said to him, 'This is what the Lord says: Because you have _____ the man I said must be _____, now you must _____ in his place, and your people will die instead of his people.'"

1 KINGS 20:42

WHAT DO I NOTICE?

Stories like this can be confusing. Why would God ask the prophet to have a friend hit him? God was going to use the prophet to teach King Ahab about obedience. It's important to stop and recognize that it is never OK to hit or hurt our friends out of anger or frustration. This is a special command by God to the prophet. His friend likely would have known this was a command by God, yet he chose to disobey. It resulted in some pretty big consequences.

What's repeated? Write down the repeated words or phrases and ask a parent or trusted Christian friend if you can circle them in your Bible!

WHAT SHOULD I DO?

Do you see any bad examples? Who and why? Do you ever act like that bad example? Explain.

PRAYER:

Spend some time thinking about today's passage and write out a prayer to God. Ask Him to help you respond in the right way.

_____

_____

_____

Today on the Journey Jr. podcast, we're talking about listening for God's voice!

TODAY'S DATE: _____

SUNDAY NOTES

_____
_____
_____
_____
_____
_____
_____
_____
_____
_____
_____
_____
_____
_____
_____
_____
_____
_____
_____
_____
_____
_____

2 KINGS

 Forgetting God's Word is the first step away from faithfulness.

HELPFUL HINTS:

- **Bible** – The written word of God

- **God is faithful** – He always keeps His promises

- **Idol** – Anything we make more important than God

- **Prayer** – Talking and listening to God

2 KINGS

1 KINGS 21:20-29

"Do you see how Ahab has humbled himself before me? Because he has done this, I will not do what I promised during his lifetime. It will happen to his sons; I will destroy his dynasty."

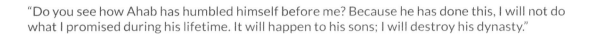

1 KINGS 21:29

WHAT DO I NOTICE?

What's happening? Draw a picture or write 3 words that describe what you read!

WHAT SHOULD I DO?

How do you see the goodness of God in this story?

Write down a truth about God you need to remember throughout your day.

PRAYER:

Spend some time thinking about today's passage and write out a prayer to God. Ask Him to help you respond in the right way.

TUESDAY | GOD USES ELIJAH
2 KINGS 1:1-17

"But Elijah replied to the captain, 'If I am a man of God, let _____ come down from heaven and destroy you and your fifty men!' Then fire fell from heaven and _____ them all."

2 KINGS 1:10

WHAT DO I NOTICE?
Who's speaking, and what do you know about them? Draw a picture of the speaker.

WHAT SHOULD I DO?
Write down a truth about God you need to remember throughout your day.

PRAYER:
Spend some time thinking about today's passage and write out a prayer to God. Ask Him to help you respond in the right way.

_____

_____

_____

_____

OCTOBER MEMORY VERSE

"Trust in the Lord with all your heart; do not depend on your own understanding. Seek his will in all you do, and he will show you which path to take." – Proverbs 3:5-6

2 KINGS 2:1-14

"When they came to the other side, Elijah said to Elisha, 'Tell me what I can do for you before I am taken away.' And Elisha replied, _____

_____

2 KINGS 2:9

WHAT DO I NOTICE?

What's happening? Draw a picture or write 3 words that describe what you read!

WHAT SHOULD I DO?

Is there a verse that stands out? If so, which one, and why do you need to remember it?

PRAYER:

Spend some time thinking about today's passage and write out a prayer to God. Ask Him to help you respond in the right way.

_____

_____

_____

2 KINGS
BIG
IDEA

Forgetting God's Word is the first step away from faithfulness.

2 KINGS 2:15-25

"Elisha left Jericho and went up to Bethel. As he was walking along the road, a group of boys from the town began mocking and making fun of him. 'Go away, baldy!' they chanted. 'Go away, baldy!'"

2 KINGS 2:23

WHAT DO I NOTICE?

What's happening? Draw a picture or write 3 words that describe what you read!

WHAT SHOULD I DO?

Do you see any bad examples? Who and why? Do you ever act like that bad example? Explain.

PRAYER:

Spend some time thinking about today's passage and write out a prayer to God. Ask Him to help you respond in the right way.

_____

_____

_____

"Trust in the Lord with all your heart; do not depend on your own understanding. Seek his will in all you do, and he will show you which path to take." – Proverbs 3:5-6

2 KINGS 4:8-17

"But sure enough, the woman soon became _____. And at that time the following year she had a _____, just as Elisha had said."

2 KINGS 4:17

WHAT DO I NOTICE?

Who's speaking, and what did they say?
Who's listening?

WHAT SHOULD I DO?

Is there someone you need to share this truth with? Who will you tell, and what would you tell them?

PRAYER:

Spend some time thinking about today's passage and write out a prayer to God. Ask Him to help you respond in the right way.

_____

_____

_____

Today on the Journey Jr. podcast: Who were Elijah and Elisha?

COLORING MAP: 2 KINGS
LET'S PLAY A GAME

Understanding the Divided Kingdom
The Nation of Israel divided in two! Israel in the North and Judah in the south.

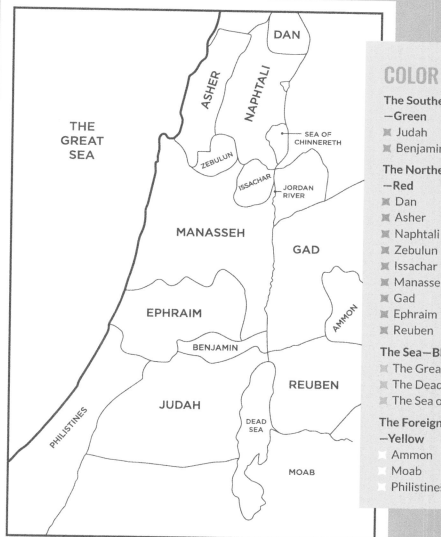

COLOR GUIDE

The Southern Kingdom —Green
- Judah
- Benjamin

The Northern Kingdom —Red
- Dan
- Asher
- Naphtali
- Zebulun
- Issachar
- Manasseh
- Gad
- Ephraim
- Reuben

The Sea—Blue
- The Great Sea
- The Dead Sea
- The Sea of Chinnereth

The Foreign Nations —Yellow
- Ammon
- Moab
- Philistines

TODAY'S DATE: _____

SUNDAY NOTES

120

2 KINGS 4:18-37

"Elisha got up, walked back and forth across the room once, and then stretched himself out again on the child. This time the boy sneezed seven times and opened his eyes!"

2 KINGS 4:35

WHAT DO I NOTICE?

What's happening? Draw a picture or write 3 words that describe what you read!

WHAT SHOULD I DO?

Do you see a good example? Is there an example to follow or instruction to obey? Explain.

PRAYER:

Spend some time thinking about today's passage and write out a prayer to God. Ask Him to help you respond in the right way.

2 KINGS BIG IDEA

Forgetting God's Word is the first step away from faithfulness.

"But the Lord did not want to destroy _____, for he had promised his servant David that his descendants would continue to _____, shining like a lamp _____."

2 KINGS 8:19

WHAT DO I NOTICE?

The book of 2 Kings alternates telling the story of all that was happening in the Northern Kingdom (that was called Israel) and the Southern Kingdom (that was called Judah). Israel did not have even one good king, but Judah had a few good kings.

Where on the Bible Timeline does this story take place?

WHAT SHOULD I DO?

Is there a promise you need to remember? If so, what is it?

PRAYER:

Spend some time thinking about today's passage and write out a prayer to God. Ask Him to help you respond in the right way.

_____

_____

_____

"Trust in the Lord with all your heart; do not depend on your own understanding. Seek his will in all you do, and he will show you which path to take." – Proverbs 3:5-6

2 KINGS 9:1-13

"You are to destroy the family of Ahab, your master.

2 KINGS 9:7

WHAT DO I NOTICE?

Who's speaking, and what did they say?
Who's listening?

WHAT SHOULD I DO?

Remember, King Ahab did not follow God at all. He did many evil things towards God and the people of Israel. We call this sin. All sin deserves to be punished, and the consequence for sin is death and separation from God. God called Jehu to wipe out Ahab's family because of their sin and how they would lead the people of Israel away from God. It is similar to what God told the Israelites before they went into the Promised Land. Though this can be hard to understand, we can remember the hope we have today in Jesus. We all are also sinners, and our sin deserves to be punished. But Jesus came and took our punishment. He died in our place so that we can be forgiven and have a new relationship with God. Think about who God is.

Write down 3 things about God you are grateful for.

PRAYER:

Spend some time thinking about today's passage and write out a prayer to God. Ask Him to help you respond in the right way.

Forgetting God's Word is the first step away from faithfulness.

2 KINGS 10:28-32

"But Jehu did not obey the Law of the Lord, the God of Israel, with all his heart. He refused to turn from the sins that Jeroboam had led Israel to commit."

2 KINGS 10:31

WHAT DO I NOTICE?
What's happening? Draw a picture or write 3 words that describe what you read!

WHAT SHOULD I DO?
Do you see any bad examples? Who and why? Do you ever act like that bad example? Explain.

PRAYER:
Spend some time thinking about today's passage and write out a prayer to God. Ask Him to help you respond in the right way.

NOVEMBER MEMORY VERSE

"Always be joyful. Never stop praying. Be thankful in all circumstances, for this is God's will for you who belong to Christ Jesus." – 1 Thessalonians 5:16-18

FRIDAY | ISRAEL IS KICKED OUT OF THEIR HOME
2 KINGS 17:6-23

"Again and again the Lord had sent his prophets and seers to warn both Israel and Judah: 'Turn from all your evil ways. Obey my commands and decrees—the entire law that I commanded your ancestors to obey, and that I gave you through my servants the prophets.' But the Israelites would not listen. They were as stubborn as their ancestors who had refused to believe in the Lord their God."

2 KINGS 17:13-14

WHAT DO I NOTICE?

Back in the Exodus Era, God gave Moses a set of commandments for the people to follow. These commandments were to show the people their need for a Savior and how to live a holy life. The people agreed to keep these commandments, and God agreed to keep this promise. We call this a covenant. God said that He would bless the people if they kept the commandments, and He would curse them if they didn't. The people at first wanted to follow God's commandments, but they quickly forgot about God and started to follow the ways of the fake gods and people around them. They disobeyed God. God gave them MANY chances to repent, or turn away from their sin, but they kept disobeying. This is why God sent the people into exile, or away from their homes. They had to face the consequences of their disobedience, but God was not going to forget about His people. He still had a plan!

How did the people respond to God?
How did God respond to the people?

WHAT SHOULD I DO?

Do you see any bad examples? Who and why? Do you ever act like that bad example? Explain.

PRAYER:

Spend some time thinking about today's passage and write out a prayer to God. Ask Him to help you respond in the right way.

_____

_____

_____

Today on the Journey Jr. podcast, we're talking all about Israel being conquered by the Assyrians.

LET'S PLAY A GAME

Why was the Northern Kingdom conquered?

This disaster came upon the people of Israel because they…

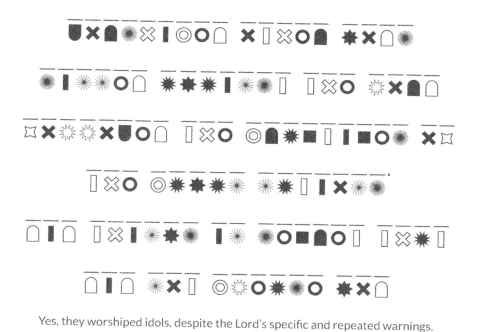

Yes, they worshiped idols, despite the Lord's specific and repeated warnings.

TODAY'S DATE: _____

SUNDAY NOTES

"He did what was pleasing in the Lord's sight, just as his ancestor David had done."

2 KINGS 18:3

WHAT DO I NOTICE?

What kind of leader was Hezekiah? List the verse numbers that explain your answer.

WHAT SHOULD I DO?

Do you see a good example? Is there an example to follow or instruction to obey? Explain.

PRAYER:

Spend some time thinking about today's passage and write out a prayer to God. Ask Him to help you respond in the right way.

2 KINGS
BIG
IDEA

Forgetting God's Word is the first step away from faithfulness.

130

2 KINGS 21:1-18

"King Manasseh of Judah has done many detestable things. He is even more wicked than the Amorites, who lived in this land before Israel. He has caused the people of Judah to sin with his idols. So this is what the Lord, the God of Israel, says: I will bring such disaster on Jerusalem and Judah that the ears of those who hear about it will tingle with horror."

2 KINGS 21:11-12

WHAT DO I NOTICE?

What kind of leader was Manasseh? List the verse numbers that explain your answer.

WHAT SHOULD I DO?

Do you see any bad examples? Who and why? Do you ever act like that bad example? Explain.

PRAYER:

Spend some time thinking about today's passage and write out a prayer to God. Ask Him to help you respond in the right way.

_____

_____

_____

"Always be joyful. Never stop praying. Be thankful in all circumstances, for this is God's will for you who belong to Christ Jesus." – 1 Thessalonians 5:16-18

2 KINGS 22:1-2, 22:8-11, 23:1-3

"The king took his place of authority beside the pillar and renewed the covenant in the Lord's presence. He pledged to obey the Lord by keeping all his commands, laws, and decrees with all his heart and soul. In this way, he confirmed all the terms of the covenant that were written in the scroll, and all the people pledged themselves to the covenant."

2 KINGS 23:3

WHAT DO I NOTICE?

How did the people respond to God?
How did God respond to the people?

WHAT SHOULD I DO?

How old was Josiah when he became king? God still wants to use young people. How might God want to use you to make His name great?

PRAYER:

Spend some time thinking about today's passage and write out a prayer to God. Ask Him to help you respond in the right way.

_____

_____

_____

2 KINGS BIG IDEA | Forgetting God's Word is the first step away from faithfulness.

2 KINGS 23:24-27, 23:31-32, 23:36-37

"For the Lord said, 'I will also banish Judah from my presence just as I have banished Israel. And I will reject my chosen city of Jerusalem and the Temple where my name was to be honored.'"

2 KINGS 23:27

WHAT DO I NOTICE?

What's repeated? Write down the repeated words or phrases and ask a parent or trusted Christian friend if you can circle them in your Bible!

WHAT SHOULD I DO?

Do you see any bad examples? Who and why? Do you ever act like that bad example? Explain.

PRAYER:

Spend some time thinking about today's passage and write out a prayer to God. Ask Him to help you respond in the right way.

_____

_____

_____

NOVEMBER MEMORY VERSE

"Always be joyful. Never stop praying. Be thankful in all circumstances, for this is God's will for you who belong to Christ Jesus." – 1 Thessalonians 5:16-18

2 KINGS 24:1-13, 25:1-7, 25:21-24

"And there at Riblah, in the land of Hamath, the king of _____ had them all put to _____. So the people of _____ were sent into _____ from their _____."

2 KINGS 25:21

WHAT DO I NOTICE?

What's happening? Draw a picture or write 3 words that describe what you read!

WHAT SHOULD I DO?

God loved the people of Israel and wanted them to turn from their sin and back to Him, but they refused. Because the Israelites worshiped other gods and sinned against the Lord, God allowed their enemies to conquer them. They were taken into captivity by Assyria and Babylon. God was still at work, though, and used prophets to send messages of hope to His people.

Do you see any bad examples? Who and why? Do you ever act like that bad example? Explain.

PRAYER:

Spend some time thinking about today's passage and write out a prayer to God. Ask Him to help you respond in the right way.

Today on the Journey Jr. podcast, we're talking all about Judah's exile.

TODAY'S DATE: _____

SUNDAY NOTES

EZRA

 Ezra set his heart to study, do, and teach the law.

HELPFUL HINTS:

- **Bible** – The written Word of God
- **Prayer** – Talking and listening to God
- **Worship** – Praising God for who He is and what He has done

EZRA

EZRA 1:1-7

"Wherever this Jewish remnant is found, let their neighbors contribute toward their expenses by giving them silver and gold, supplies for the journey, and livestock, as well as a voluntary offering for the Temple of God in Jerusalem."

EZRA 1:4

WHAT DO I NOTICE?

Finally! The Israelites were able to return to their home! Many years passed between the events recorded in 2 Kings and the events we read about in Ezra. Now in today's reading, Jeremiah is mentioned. The book of Jeremiah was written many, many years before the events we read about today took place. Remember, prophets were messengers God used to communicate His direction to His people. When we study the Bible, it's important to ask the question, "What else does the Bible say about this?"

Take a look at Jeremiah 25:11-12. What 4 things did God say would happen?

WHAT SHOULD I DO?

God keeps His word! He never goes back on what He says. Because of this fact, we can call God a "promise keeper."

Have you ever broken a promise? Have you ever said one thing and done something different? How would God have wanted you to respond?

REMINDER TO ORDER

Uh-oh! You're going to run out of pages soon!
Ask a parent or trusted Christian friend to help you order a new journal!

EZRA 3:1-13

"With praise and thanks, they sang this song to the Lord: 'He is so _____! His faithful love for Israel endures _____!' Then all the people gave a great shout, praising the Lord because the foundation of the Lord's _____ had been laid."

EZRA 3:11

WHAT DO I NOTICE?

Remember, when the Babylonians conquered the Israelites in Judah, the temple was destroyed. Now, God's people are working to rebuild it!

What's happening? Draw a picture or write 3 words that describe what you read!

WHAT SHOULD I DO?

Write down a truth about God you need to remember throughout your day.

PRAYER:

Spend some time thinking about today's passage and write out a prayer to God. Ask Him to help you respond in the right way.

_____

_____

_____

NOVEMBER MEMORY VERSE

"Always be joyful. Never stop praying. Be thankful in all circumstances, for this is God's will for you who belong to Christ Jesus." – 1 Thessalonians 5:16-18

EZRA 6:6-18

"The Temple of God was then dedicated _____

_____

WHAT DO I NOTICE?

Who's speaking, and what did they say?
Who's listening?

WHAT SHOULD I DO?

Do you see a good example? Is there an example to follow or instruction to obey? Explain.

PRAYER:

Spend some time thinking about today's passage and write out a prayer to God. Ask Him to help you respond in the right way.

_____

_____

_____

EZRA
BIG
IDEA

Ezra set his heart to study, do, and teach the law.

"This was because Ezra had determined to study and obey the Law of the Lord and to teach those decrees and regulations to the people of Israel."

EZRA 7:10

WHAT DO I NOTICE?

Ezra was an important leader for Israel. His job was to remind the Israelites of the law: God's instructions for His people.

What kinds of things did Ezra do? Make a list and see how many you can count!

What's repeated? (Hint: the word you're looking for starts with the letter "G.")

WHAT SHOULD I DO?

Do you see a good example? Is there an example to follow or instruction to obey? Explain.

PRAYER:

Spend some time thinking about today's passage and write out a prayer to God. Ask Him to help you respond in the right way.

_____

_____

_____

NOVEMBER MEMORY VERSE

"Always be joyful. Never stop praying. Be thankful in all circumstances, for this is God's will for you who belong to Christ Jesus." – 1 Thessalonians 5:16-18

EZRA 9:10-15, 10:1-2

"O Lord, God of Israel, you are _____. We come before you in our _____ as nothing but an escaped remnant, though in such a condition _____ of us can stand in your _____."

EZRA 9:15

WHAT DO I NOTICE?

How did the people respond to God?
How did God respond to the people?

WHAT SHOULD I DO?

Do you see any bad examples? Who and why? Do you ever act like that bad example? Explain.

PRAYER:

Spend some time thinking about today's passage and write out a prayer to God. Ask Him to help you respond in the right way.

_____

_____

_____

Today on the podcast, we're doing an overview of Ezra's leadership!

LET'S PLAY A GAME

What did Ezra do?

"$\underline{\;5\;26\;18\;1\;}$ $\underline{\;8\;1\;4\;}$ $\underline{\;4\;5\;20\;5\;18\;13\;9\;14\;5\;4\;}$ $\underline{\;20\;15\;}$

$\underline{\;19\;20\;21\;4\;25\;}$ $\underline{\;1\;14\;4\;}$ $\underline{\;15\;2\;5\;25\;}$ $\underline{\;20\;8\;5\;}$ $\underline{\;12\;1\;23\;15\;6\;}$

$\underline{\;20\;8\;5\;}$ $\underline{\;12\;15\;18\;4\;}$ $\underline{\;1\;14\;4\;}$ $\underline{\;20\;15\;}$ $\underline{\;20\;5\;1\;3\;8\;}$ $\underline{\;20\;8\;15\;19\;5\;}$

$\underline{\;4\;5\;3\;18\;5\;5\;19\;}$ $\underline{\;1\;14\;4\;}$ $\underline{\;18\;5\;7\;21\;12\;1\;20\;9\;15\;14\;19\;}$

$\underline{\;20\;15\;}$ $\underline{\;20\;8\;5\;}$ $\underline{\;16\;5\;15\;16\;12\;5\;}$ $\underline{\;15\;6\;}$ $\underline{\;9\;19\;18\;1\;5\;12\;}$."

A — 1	E — 5	I — 9	M — 13	Q — 17	U — 21	Y — 25
B — 2	F — 6	J — 10	N — 14	R — 18	V — 22	Z — 26
C — 3	G — 7	K — 11	O — 15	S — 19	W — 23	
D — 4	H — 8	L — 12	P — 16	T — 20	X — 24	

SUNDAY NOTES

NEHEMIAH

 Start with prayer.

HELPFUL HINTS:

- **Prayer** – Talking and listening to God
- **Glory** – God's perfect goodness and greatness
- **Sin** – Anything we think, say, or do that does not please or honor God
- **Idol** – Anything we make more important than God

NEHEMIAH

"They said to me, 'Things are not going well for those who returned to the province of Judah. They are in great trouble and disgrace. The wall of Jerusalem has been torn down, and the gates have been destroyed by fire.'"

NEHEMIAH 1:3

WHAT DO I NOTICE?

As the Israelites returned home from Babylon, they came in waves, or different groups. Nehemiah recorded all that happened with the third group of Israelites returning home. During the first wave, we saw that the temple was reconstructed, and the people were reminded of the law (thanks to Ezra!). Now we are going to see God's people rebuild the wall around their city while under Nehemiah's leadership!

What's happening? Draw a picture or write 3 words that describe what you read!

WHAT SHOULD I DO?

Do you see a good example? Is there an example to follow or instruction to obey? Explain.

PRAYER:

Spend some time thinking about today's passage and write out a prayer to God. Ask Him to help you respond in the right way.

_____

_____

_____

NEHEMIAH
BIG
IDEA

Start with prayer.

"I replied, 'If it please the king, and if you are pleased with me, your servant, send me to

_____ to _____ the _____ where my ancestors are buried.'"

NEHEMIAH 2:5

WHAT DO I NOTICE?
Who's speaking, and what did they say? Who's listening?

WHAT SHOULD I DO?
Is there a verse that stands out? If so, which one, and why do you need to remember it?

PRAYER:
Spend some time thinking about today's passage and write out a prayer to God. Ask Him to help you respond in the right way.

_____

_____

_____

"Always be joyful. Never stop praying. Be thankful in all circumstances, for this is God's will for you who belong to Christ Jesus." – 1 Thessalonians 5:16-18

NEHEMIAH 4:1-15

"At last the wall was _____

_____

WHAT DO I NOTICE?

What's happening? Draw a picture or write 3 words that describe what you read!

WHAT SHOULD I DO?

Do you see any bad examples? Who and why? Do you ever act like that bad example? Explain.

PRAYER:

Spend some time thinking about today's passage and write out a prayer to God. Ask Him to help you respond in the right way.

_____

_____

_____

NEHEMIAH
BIG
IDEA

Start with prayer.

NEHEMIAH 5:9-19

"Then I pressed further, 'What you are doing is not right! Should you not walk in the fear of our God in order to avoid being mocked by enemy nations?'"

NEHEMIAH 5:9

WHAT DO I NOTICE?

Who's speaking, and what did they say? Who's listening?

WHAT SHOULD I DO?

Do you see any bad examples? Who and why? Do you ever act like that bad example? Explain.

PRAYER:

Spend some time thinking about today's passage and write out a prayer to God. Ask Him to help you respond in the right way.

_____

_____

_____

NOVEMBER MEMORY VERSE

"Always be joyful. Never stop praying. Be thankful in all circumstances, for this is God's will for you who belong to Christ Jesus." – 1 Thessalonians 5:16-18

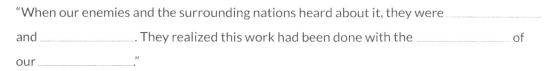

NEHEMIAH 6:1-16

"When our enemies and the surrounding nations heard about it, they were _____ and _____. They realized this work had been done with the _____ of our _____."

NEHEMIAH 6:16

WHAT DO I NOTICE?

Who's speaking, and what did they say? Who's listening?

WHAT SHOULD I DO?

Do you see any bad examples? Who and why? Do you ever act like that bad example? Explain.

PRAYER:

Spend some time thinking about today's passage and write out a prayer to God. Ask Him to help you respond in the right way.

_____

_____

_____

Today on the podcast, we're talking all about opposition throughout the rebuilding of the wall of Jerusalem!

SUNDAY NOTES

NEHEMIAH 8:1-12

"They read from the Book of the Law of God and clearly explained the meaning of what was being read, helping the people understand each passage."

NEHEMIAH 8:8

WHAT DO I NOTICE?

What's happening? Draw a picture or write 3 words that describe what you read!

WHAT SHOULD I DO?

Write down a truth about God you need to remember throughout your day.

PRAYER:

Spend some time thinking about today's passage and write out a prayer to God. Ask Him to help you respond in the right way.

NEHEMIAH
BIG
IDEA

Start with prayer.

NEHEMIAH 9:3-8, 9:29-38

"They remained standing in place for _____ hours while the Book of the Law of the Lord their God was _____ aloud to them. Then for three more hours they _____ their sins and _____ the Lord their God."

NEHEMIAH 9:3

WHAT DO I NOTICE?

What's repeated? Write down the repeated words or phrases and ask a parent or trusted Christian friend if you can circle them in your Bible!

WHAT SHOULD I DO?

Is there someone you need to share this truth with? Who will you tell, and what would you tell them?

PRAYER:

Spend some time thinking about today's passage and write out a prayer to God. Ask Him to help you respond in the right way.

_____

_____

_____

NOVEMBER MEMORY VERSE

"Always be joyful. Never stop praying. Be thankful in all circumstances, for this is God's will for you who belong to Christ Jesus." – 1 Thessalonians 5:16-18

NEHEMIAH 10:28-39

"They swore a curse on themselves if they failed to obey the Law of God _____

_____

_____

NEHEMIAH 10:29B

WHAT DO I NOTICE?

What's repeated? How many times does the repeated word or phrase appear in this passage?

WHAT SHOULD I DO?

Do you see a good example? Is there an example to follow or instruction to obey? Explain.

PRAYER:

Spend some time thinking about today's passage and write out a prayer to God. Ask Him to help you respond in the right way.

_____

_____

_____

NEHEMIAH
BIG
IDEA

Start with prayer.

THURSDAY | WORSHIP GOD FOR ALL HE'S DONE!
NEHEMIAH 12:27-43

"Many sacrifices were offered on that joyous day, for God had given the people cause for great joy. The women and children also participated in the celebration, and the joy of the people of Jerusalem could be heard far away."

NEHEMIAH 12:43

WHAT DO I NOTICE?
Where is this story taking place? Draw a picture of the setting.

WHAT SHOULD I DO?
Do you see a good example? Is there an example to follow or instruction to obey? Explain.

PRAYER:
Spend some time thinking about today's passage and write out a prayer to God. Ask Him to help you respond in the right way.

NOVEMBER MEMORY VERSE | "Always be joyful. Never stop praying. Be thankful in all circumstances, for this is God's will for you who belong to Christ Jesus." – 1 Thessalonians 5:16-18

NEHEMIAH 13:6-7, 13:10-22

"I immediately confronted the leaders and demanded, 'Why has the Temple of God been

_____?' Then I called all the _____ back again and _____ them

to their proper duties."

NEHEMIAH 13:11

WHAT DO I NOTICE?

While Nehemiah was out of town, the people returned to their old ways and were not honoring God! You would think that, after all this time, after facing lots of consequences for their sins and getting lots of reminders, they'd make good choices. Unfortunately, the Israelites went back to their poor choices. Even though they promised God they were going to make good choices, they still chose their sinful ways. Ultimately, the Israelites found themselves left in silence. For 400 years, God did not send another prophet or messenger. They simply waited. Nehemiah is the last historical book of the Old Testament.

What's happening? Draw a picture or write 3 words that describe what you read!

WHAT SHOULD I DO?

Do you see any bad examples? Who and why? Do you ever act like that bad example? Explain.

PRAYER:

Spend some time thinking about today's passage and write out a prayer to God. Ask Him to help you respond in the right way.

_____

_____

_____

Today on the podcast we're exploring how God's people respond. Are they faithful?

TODAY'S DATE: _____

SUNDAY NOTES

ADVENT

 God with us.

HELPFUL HINTS:

- **God** – The all-powerful, all-knowing, all-seeing Creator of everything
- **Glory** – God's perfect goodness and greatness
- **God is faithful** – He always keeps His promises
- **Worship** – Praising God for who He is and What He has done

ADVENT

JOHN 1:1-18

"In the beginning the Word already existed. The Word was with God, and the Word was God."

JOHN 1:1

WHAT DO I NOTICE?

What did you learn about God from these verses? List 4 things!

WHAT SHOULD I DO?

Write down a truth about God you need to remember throughout your day.

PRAYER:

Spend some time thinking about today's passage and write out a prayer to God. Ask Him to help you respond in the right way.

ADVENT
BIG
IDEA

God with us.

GENESIS 1:1-2, 1:26-28, 3:1-15

"And I will cause _____ between you and the woman, and between your _____

and her offspring. He will strike your _____, and you will strike his _____."

GENESIS 3:15

WHAT DO I NOTICE?

What's happening? Draw a picture or write 3 words that describe what you read!

WHAT SHOULD I DO?

Is there a promise you need to remember? If so, what is it?

PRAYER:

Spend some time thinking about today's passage and write out a prayer to God. Ask Him to help you respond in the right way.

_____

_____

_____

DECEMBER MEMORY VERSE

"Create in me a clean heart, O God.
Renew a loyal spirit within me." – Psalm 51:10

GENESIS 12:1-3; DEUT. 18:18; ACTS 3:17-26

"I will raise up a prophet like you _____

_____

_____

DEUTERONOMY 18:18

WHAT DO I NOTICE?

Where on the Bible Timeline do these 3 passages occur?

What did God say to Abraham?

WHAT SHOULD I DO?

Is there a verse that stands out? If so, which one, and why do you need to remember it?

PRAYER:

Spend some time thinking about today's passage and write out a prayer to God. Ask Him to help you respond in the right way.

_____

_____

_____

ADVENT
BIG
IDEA

God with us.

GENESIS 17:15-19; ROMANS 9:1-13

"But God replied, 'No—Sarah, your wife, will give birth to a son for you. You will name him Isaac, and I will confirm my covenant with him and his descendants as an everlasting covenant.'"

GENESIS 17:19

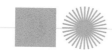

WHAT DO I NOTICE?

What did you learn about God from these verses? List 4 things!

WHAT SHOULD I DO?

Write down a truth about God you need to remember throughout your day.

PRAYER:

Spend some time thinking about today's passage and write out a prayer to God. Ask Him to help you respond in the right way.

_____

_____

_____

REMINDER TO ORDER

Uh-oh! You're almost out of pages!
Ask a parent or trusted Christian friend to help you order a new journal!

"He is the one who will build a _____—a _____—for my name. And I will secure his royal _____ _____."

2 SAMUEL 7:13

WHAT DO I NOTICE?

Where on the Bible Timeline do these 3 passages occur?

What's repeated? Write down the repeated words or phrases and ask a parent or trusted Christian friend if you can circle them in your Bible!

WHAT SHOULD I DO?

Is there a promise you need to remember? If so, what is it?

PRAYER:

Spend some time thinking about today's passage and write out a prayer to God. Ask Him to help you respond in the right way.

_____

_____

_____

Today on the podcast: How do we know Jesus was God's plan A?

CROSSWORD: IT'S CHRISTMAS TIME!
LET'S PLAY A GAME

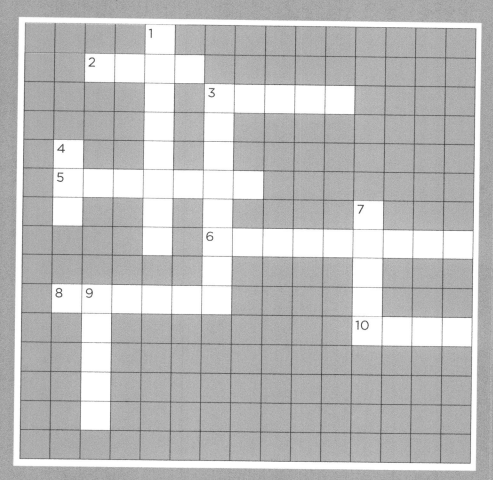

ACROSS

2. Who was Jesus's mom?
3. Jesus was a descendant of this great king!
5. Who came from the east to visit Jesus?
6. In what city was Jesus born?
8. Where did Jesus sleep after he was born?
10. What led the Wise Men to Jesus?

DOWN

1. Jesus fulfilled _____.
3. We celebrate Christmas in what month of the year?
4. We read about Jesus's birth in this chapter of Luke.
7. Whose birth does Christmas celebrate?
9. What appeared to Mary?

SUNDAY NOTES

ISAIAH 9:2-7; MATT. 1:1-17

"For a child is born to us, a son is given to us. The government will rest on his shoulders. And he will be called: Wonderful Counselor, Mighty God, Everlasting Father, Prince of Peace."

ISAIAH 9:6

WHAT DO I NOTICE?

There's a long list of names in Matthew 1. In your Bible, underline each name the FIRST time it appears. Then record a list of the names you recognize below.

What do you know about those people?

WHAT SHOULD I DO?

Is there a promise you need to remember? If so, what is it?

PRAYER:

Spend some time thinking about today's passage and write out a prayer to God. Ask Him to help you respond in the right way.

Uh-oh! You're almost out of pages!
Ask a parent or trusted Christian friend to help you order a new journal!

ISAIAH 7:14; LUKE 1:6-7, 1:11-45

"He will be very _____ and will be called the Son of the Most High. The Lord God will give

him the _____ of his ancestor David. And he will _____ over Israel forever; his

Kingdom will _____ end!"

LUKE 1:32-33

WHAT DO I NOTICE?

What's happening? Draw a picture or write 3 words that describe what you read!

WHAT SHOULD I DO?

Do you see a good example? Is there an example to follow or instruction to obey? Explain.

PRAYER:

Spend some time thinking about today's passage and write out a prayer to God. Ask Him to help you respond in the right way.

_____

_____

_____

DECEMBER MEMORY VERSE

"Create in me a clean heart, O God.
Renew a loyal spirit within me." – Psalm 51:10

171

LUKE 1:46-56

"He has helped his servant Israel _____

_____

_____

LUKE 1:54-55

WHAT DO I NOTICE?

Who's speaking, and what do you know about them? Draw a picture of the speaker.

WHAT SHOULD I DO?

Is there a verse that stands out? If so, which one, and why do you need to remember it?

PRAYER:

Spend some time thinking about today's passage and write out a prayer to God. Ask Him to help you respond in the right way.

_____

_____

_____

ADVENT
BIG
IDEA

God with us.

THURSDAY | CHRIST IS BORN
LUKE 2:1-7

"And while they were there, the time came for her baby to be born. She gave birth to her firstborn son. She wrapped him snugly in strips of cloth and laid him in a manger, because there was no lodging available for them."

LUKE 2:6-7

WHAT DO I NOTICE?

What's happening? Draw a picture or write 3 words that describe what you read!

WHAT SHOULD I DO?

Is there someone you need to share this truth with? Who will you tell, and what would you tell them?

PRAYER:

Spend some time thinking about today's passage and write out a prayer to God. Ask Him to help you respond in the right way.

_____

_____

_____

DECEMBER MEMORY VERSE

"Create in me a clean heart, O God.
Renew a loyal spirit within me." – Psalm 51:10

173

FRIDAY | CHRIST IS BORN
LUKE 2:8-12

"The _____ —yes, the _____ , the Lord—has been _____ today in Bethlehem, the city of David!"

LUKE 2:11

WHAT DO I NOTICE?

Where is this story taking place? Draw a picture of the setting.

WHAT SHOULD I DO?

How should we respond to the good news of Jesus's birth?

PRAYER:

Spend some time thinking about today's passage and write out a prayer to God. Ask Him to help you respond in the right way.

Today on the podcast, we're talking all about the birth of Christ!

HELP MARY AND JOSEPH TRAVEL FROM NAZARETH TO BETHLEHEM!

LET'S PLAY A GAME

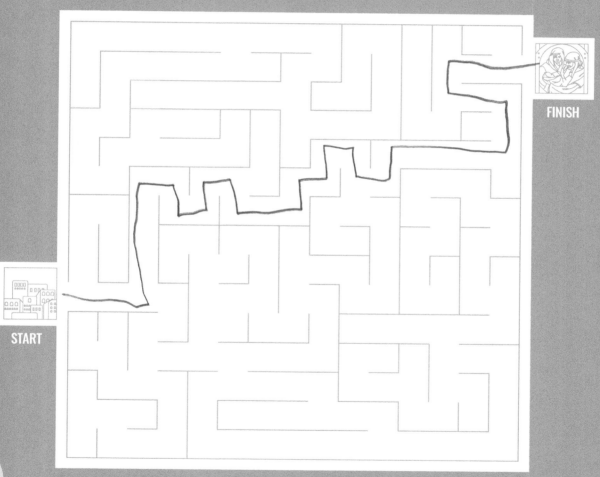

FINISH

START

SUNDAY NOTES

LUKE 2:13-18

"When the angels had returned to heaven, the shepherds said to each other, 'Let's go to Bethlehem! Let's see this thing that has happened, which the Lord has told us about.'"

LUKE 2:15

WHAT DO I NOTICE?

What's happening? Draw a picture or write 3 words that describe what you read!

WHAT SHOULD I DO?

Do you see a good example? Is there an example to follow or instruction to obey? Explain.

PRAYER:

Spend some time thinking about today's passage and write out a prayer to God. Ask Him to help you respond in the right way.

ADVENT
BIG
IDEA

God with us.

TUESDAY | CHRIST IS BORN
LUKE 2:19-20

"The shepherds went back to their flocks, _____ and _____ God for all they had heard and seen. It was just as the _____ had told them."

LUKE 2:20

WHAT DO I NOTICE?
How did the people respond to God?
How did God respond to the people?

WHAT SHOULD I DO?
Do you see a good example? Is there an example to follow or instruction to obey? Explain.

PRAYER:
Spend some time thinking about today's passage and write out a prayer to God. Ask Him to help you respond in the right way.

_____

_____

_____

REMINDER TO ORDER

Uh-oh! You're almost out of pages!
Ask a parent or trusted Christian friend to help you order a new journal!

MICAH 5:2-5

"But you, O Bethlehem Ephrathah, _____
_____
_____

MICAH 5:2

WHAT DO I NOTICE?
Make a timeline of the events the prophet said would unfold.

WHAT SHOULD I DO?
Is there anything you read that you don't understand? If so, ask a parent or trusted Christian friend for help!

PRAYER:
Spend some time thinking about today's passage and write out a prayer to God. Ask Him to help you respond in the right way.

_____
_____
_____

ADVENT
BIG
IDEA

God with us.

MICAH 5:2; MATTHEW 2:1-6

"And you, O Bethlehem in the land of Judah, are not least among the ruling cities of Judah, for a ruler will come from you who will be the shepherd for my people Israel.'"

MATTHEW 2:6

WHAT DO I NOTICE?

Who's speaking, and what did they say? Who's listening?

WHAT SHOULD I DO?

Is there a verse that stands out? If so, which one, and why do you need to remember it?

PRAYER:

Spend some time thinking about today's passage and write out a prayer to God. Ask Him to help you respond in the right way.

DECEMBER MEMORY VERSE

"Create in me a clean heart, O God. Renew a loyal spirit within me." – Psalm 51:10

"After this interview the wise men went their way. And the _____ they had seen in the east guided them to Bethlehem. It went _____ of them and _____ over the place where the child was."

MATTHEW 2:9

WHAT DO I NOTICE?

What's happening? Draw a picture or write 3 words that describe what you read!

WHAT SHOULD I DO?

Do you see a good example? Is there an example to follow or instruction to obey? Explain.

PRAYER:

Spend some time thinking about today's passage and write out a prayer to God. Ask Him to help you respond in the right way.

_____

_____

_____

What does it mean that Christ came to fulfill the law?
We're talking all about Jesus on this week's podcast episode.

LET'S PLAY A GAME

One of the first times we read about Jesus in our Bibles...

"
___ ___ ___   ___   ___ ___ ___ ___   ___ ___ ___   ___ ___ ___ ___ ___ ___
1 14 4   9   23 9 12 12   16 21 20   19 20 18 9 6 5

___ ___ ___ ___ ___ ___ ___   ___ ___ ___   ___ ___ ___   ___ ___ ___   ___ ___ ___ ___ ___,
2 5 20 23 5 5 14   25 15 21   1 14 4   20 8 5   23 15 13 1 14

___ ___ ___   ___ ___ ___ ___ ___ ___ ___   ___ ___ ___ ___
1 14 4   2 5 20 23 5 5 14   25 15 21 18

___ ___ ___ ___ ___ ___ ___ ___ ___   ___ ___ ___   ___ ___ ___ ___;
15 6 6 19 16 18 9 14 7   1 14 4   8 5 18 19

___ ___   ___ ___ ___ ___   ___ ___ ___ ___ ___   ___ ___ ___ ___   ___ ___ ___ ___,
8 5   23 9 12 12   3 18 21 19 8   25 15 21 18   8 5 1 4

___ ___ ___   ___ ___ ___   ___ ___ ___ ___   ___ ___ ___ ___ ___ ___
1 14 4   25 15 21   23 9 12 12   19 20 18 9 11 5
"
___ ___ ___   ___ ___ ___ ___.
8 9 19   8 5 5 12

A — 1	E — 5	I — 9	M — 13	Q — 17	U — 21	Y — 25
B — 2	F — 6	J — 10	N — 14	R — 18	V — 22	Z — 26
C — 3	G — 7	K — 11	O — 15	S — 19	W — 23	
D — 4	H — 8	L — 12	P — 16	T — 20	X — 24	

SUNDAY NOTES

LUKE 2:11-14

"Suddenly, the angel was joined by a vast host of others—the armies of heaven—praising God and saying, 'Glory to God in highest heaven, and peace on earth to those with whom God is pleased.'"

LUKE 2:13-14

WHAT DO I NOTICE?

Where on the Bible Timeline does this story take place?

WHAT SHOULD I DO?

Do you see a good example? Is there an example to follow or instruction to obey? Explain.

PRAYER:

Spend some time thinking about today's passage and write out a prayer to God. Ask Him to help you respond in the right way.

_____

_____

_____

ADVENT
BIG
IDEA

God with us.

REVELATION 1:4-7

"'I am the _____ and the _____—the beginning and the end,' says the Lord God.
'I am the one who _____, who always _____, and who is still to _____
—the Almighty One.'"

REVELATION 1:8

WHAT DO I NOTICE?

Where on the Bible Timeline does this story take place?

What did you learn about God from these verses? List 4 things!

WHAT SHOULD I DO?

Write down a truth about God you need to remember throughout your day.

PRAYER:

Spend some time thinking about today's passage and write out a prayer to God. Ask Him to help you respond in the right way.

_____

_____

_____

DECEMBER MEMORY VERSE

"Create in me a clean heart, O God.
Renew a loyal spirit within me." – Psalm 51:10

REVELATION 3:20-22

"Look! I stand at the door and knock. _____
_____
_____

REVELATION 3:20

WHAT DO I NOTICE?

Who's speaking, and what did they say?
Who's listening?

WHAT SHOULD I DO?

Is there instruction you can apply to
your own life? If so, what is it?

PRAYER:

Spend some time thinking about today's passage and write out a prayer to God. Ask Him to help
you respond in the right way.

_____

_____

_____

ADVENT
BIG
IDEA

God with us.

REVELATION 22:12-13

"I am the Alpha and the Omega, the First and the Last, the Beginning and the End."

REVELATION 22:13

WHAT DO I NOTICE?

Who's speaking, and what did they say?
Who's listening?

WHAT SHOULD I DO?

Write down a truth about God you need
to remember throughout your day.

PRAYER:

Spend some time thinking about today's passage and write out a prayer to God. Ask Him to help
you respond in the right way.

REMINDER TO ORDER

Uh-oh! You're almost out of pages!
Ask a parent or trusted Christian friend to help you order a new journal!

"I, Jesus, have sent my angel to give you this message for the churches. I am both the _____ of David and the _____ to his throne. I am the bright morning star."

REVELATION 22:16

WHAT DO I NOTICE?

Who's speaking, and what did they say? Who's listening?

WHAT SHOULD I DO?

Is there instruction you can apply to your own life? If so, what is it?

PRAYER:

Spend some time thinking about today's passage and write out a prayer to God. Ask Him to help you respond in the right way.

_____

_____

_____

Why is Jesus the Savior of the world? We're talking all about Christ's return on today's podcast episode!

TODAY'S DATE: _____

SUNDAY NOTES

_____
_____
_____
_____
_____
_____
_____
_____
_____
_____
_____
_____
_____
_____
_____
_____
_____
_____
_____
_____